ABOUT HORWICH

by

M.D. Smith

in collaboration with
John Smith & Martin Brownlow

Dedicated to the memory of John Rawlinson (author of 'About Rivington') –
11.4.1903 to 26.2.1972.

Still o'er these scenes my memory wakes,
And fondly broods with miser care!
Time but the impression stronger makes,
As streams their channels deeper wear.

Robert Burns

ISBN 0 9508772 7 1

Printed & Published by Nelson Brothers Printers Limited
Fellery Street, Chorley, Lancs PR7 1EJ

Lee Lane, Horwich – 1902. This photograph shows the celebrations for the Coronation of King Edward VII. The horse drawn vehicle to the right was used as a 'Black Maria'/Ambulance/Fever Wagon and was stored behind the Public Hall.

ACKNOWLEDGEMENTS

My first duty is to record sincere thanks for the generous help and expert guidance afforded me by John Smith, Harts Houses, Horwich, and for the equally unselfish assistance of Martin Brownlow, Brownlow Road, Horwich. Without their co-operation the publication of this work would not have been possible.

My thanks are also due to my wife Andrea for typing and checking the manuscript.

The persons listed below have also provided valuable assistance which I have been grateful to receive and am pleased to acknowledge:–

Jill M Aldersley – North Road, Ambleside, Cumbria (Front Cover)
Joan Birchall – Foxholes, Horwich
Ernest Bosworth – Fleet Street, Horwich (Back Cover)
Edward Brownlow – Brownlow Road, Horwich
Mary Harrison – Fleet Street, Horwich
Eileen and Gordon Kay – Victoria Road, Horwich
Neil Kealing – Bolton Evening News
Ida Mason – Babylon Lane, Anderton
Norman Pendlebury – Darley Street, Horwich
Norman Carlton Slark, Hough Fold Way, Harwood, Bolton
Horwich Town Council

INTRODUCTION

'About Horwich' is intended to be just what the title implies, a book about the town, its environs and its people.

The rich history of the place has made it more difficult to decide on what not to include rather than the actual contents. However, working on the adage that – 'the person who fails to make a decision rarely makes anything' – the text and illustrations included have been decided upon. Apologies are tendered in advance for anything left out. It is not possible in an undertaking of this size to cover each and every aspect of the town's historical past. Nevertheless, it is hoped that the result will prove both interesting and informative.

While researching this work I came across the following quote which expresses, far more eloquently than I am able to, the reason for taking on this project in the first place:-

"The poetry of history lies in the quasi-maraculous fact that, once, on this earth, on this familiar spot of ground, walked other men and women, as actual as we are today, thinking their own thoughts, swayed by their own passions, but now all gone, one generation vanishing after another, gone as utterly as ourselves will shortly be gone, like ghosts at cock-crow". (G M Trevelyan).

M D Smith – Adlington, Lancashire. 1987.

CONTENTS

CHAPTER 1
Early Settlers in the Horwich District

It is ironic that some of the most interesting discoveries providing evidence of early settlers in the Horwich District have only been made during the last fifty years.

In 1946 just after the Second World War, Mr Southworth of Anderton was out walking near the Horwich/Rivington boundary, in the valley of the River Douglas at a place known locally as 'Tiger's Clough'; when he noticed an unusual shaped stone in the river bed. On retrieving the stone which was roughly six inches long he saw that it had been fashioned into an axe-head and the surface was polished smooth. Not realising the full significance of the find, Mr Southworth took the axe-head home in his pocket and placed it at one side as a curio.

Tiger's Clough Horwich – (Circa 1910). The photograph was taken by Ralph Close of Horwich whose daughter is standing on the bridge.

1

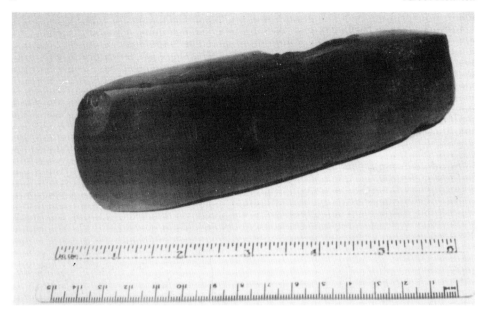

Scandinavian axe-head dating from 2,500 B.C. found in Tiger's Clough Horwich in 1946.

Despite the fact that this axe-head was one of only two ever to have been found in the British Isles, the other one having been unearthed in Cambridgeshire, it was not until 1962, some sixteen years after the discovery, that a relative of Mr Southworth was prevailed upon to have the axe-head expertly examined.

Professor D F Petch a Fellow of the Society of Antiquaries carried out a petrological survey of the axe-head and reported that it dated from the Neolithic or Polished Stone-Age period, about 2,500 B.C. It was of Scandinavian stone and similar in design to examples found in Scandinavia.

In isolation the axe-head is not positive proof of trade with Scandinavia or of Scandinavians visiting the area or settling here. Nevertheless the axe-head was an intriguing discovery and caused a mild sensation at the time.

The existence of Bronze Age settlements in the Horwich area has been more conclusively established and once again the discovery was made by pure chance. On the 24th March 1957, two old friends, John Rawlinson and Tom Creear, were out together walking on Winter Hill when they noticed a curved line of stones protruding from the moorland soil. John was a local historian of some note and, appreciating the importance of the chance discovery, made a further examination of the site. The stones formed part of a wall some 25 inches in height and this wall enclosed a circular area 63 feet in diameter which was mounded at the centre. The details and location of the mound were reported to Mr C E P Rosser of Manchester University.

On the 6th August 1957, Mr Rosser accompanied by two colleagues from Manchester University visited Winter

Hill to see the circle of stones. Following a preliminary examination he decided that this was a Bronze Age Barrow or burial mound and a decision was taken to excavate the site during the following summer. Commencing on the 18th July 1958, a portion of the centre of the Winter Hill Barrow was excavated but, unfortunately, it soon became obvious that the burial mound had already been dug, approximately 250 years previously. Nevertheless the Winter Hill dig continued for two weeks and analysis of pollen taken from the grave positively dated the structure as Middle Bronze Age, about 1500 B.C.

measuring about two feet six inches long by one foot wide by eight inches deep, and an inner ring of smaller stones strengthened by buttresses. These walls formed two concentric circles with diameters of 52 feet and 33 feet respectively. Within the smaller circle two heaps of burned bones and a cremation urn were found suggesting three human burials.

Other finds included two tanged and barbed flint arrowheads along with a sacrificial flint knife with one conventional cutting side to the blade and a saw toothed side. The artefacts dated the erection of the Noon Hill Saucer Tumulus at around 1100 B.C.

Tom Creear.

John Rawlinson.

In August 1958, members of the Bolton and District Archeological Society, led by John Winstanley, excavated the Noon Hill Saucer Tumulus which is situated half a mile west of Winter Hill. A quadrant of the Tumulus was removed disclosing an outer ring of large stones

There are other prominences on the moorland above Horwich which are indicative of Bronze Age habitation. The Pike Stones on Anglezarke Moor are believed to be a Megalithic Tomb and Round Loaf on the same moor has the appearance of a large tumulus.

Midlands Forensic Science Laboratory to use it in research. That may well have been the end of the story but for the persistence of Alderman C Williams of Queens Road, Chorley, a founder of the Chorley Archeological Society, who successfully re-located the skull after an 11 year search. (Mr Williams was also involved in the Winter Hill dig).

A rotary top quern stone for use in grinding corn, and dating from the first century A.D. was recovered on Red Moss and is presently exhibited in Bolton Museum.

The Red Moss peat bog lying in the natural valley between Horwich and Blackrod has also yielded its share of secrets concerning early inhabitants. In 1942 while working on the moss near to the Blackrod boundary a peat cutter named Krikken came across a human skull. This grisly find was duly reported to the local constabulary and a forensic examination was carried out to establish whether or not a murder hunt should be launched. In the event, the skull was identified as that of a red haired female, aged approximately 30 years, who had died some 3,000 years previously, about 1058 B.C.

After interest had waned in the incident, the landowner on whose property the skull was found gave permission for a

Excavation of the Winter Hill Burial Mound in July 1958. The man pointing is Charles Williams, a Chorley Alderman who was President of the Archaeological Society.

Rotary top quern stone found on the Red Moss, Horwich.

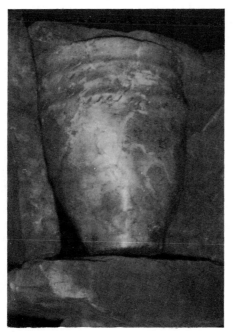

Cinerary Urn from the Noon-Hill Saucer Tumulus dated 1100 B.C. (Presently on display in Bolton Museum).

CHAPTER 2
'Dwellers in a land of many waters'.

1830 engraving of Horwich from Blackrod with Rivington Pike in the background.

The first incursions made by the Roman legions under Julius Caeser in B.C. 55 and 54 were principally reconnaissance missions and the actual Romanisation of Britain did not begin in earnest until the invasion made in A.D 43. It was not until A.D. 79 that the Brigantes,

a fierce warlike tribe who occupied all the country north of the River Humber, finally submitted to the superior Roman forces under General Julius Agricola. At this time the whole of the area of what prior to 1974 was Lancashire consisted of dense forest, moorland and bogland.

6

The inhabitants of the area who had resisted the Roman invaders for so long, fighting from places of refuge in the Pennine Chain were known to the Romans as the 'Segantii' or 'dwellers in a land of many waters'.

Horwich cannot claim any notable connection with the period of Roman occupation but neighbouring Blackrod is mentioned in several publications as being the site of the Roman Station – 'Coccium'. This theory has since been disproved and it has long been thought that the title correctly belongs to Wigan. However, archaeological excavations being carried out in Wigan town centre at the time of writing, have produced fresh evidence of the Roman era which, it is understood, dispute this belief. Nevertheless there does seem to have been a small

Roman fort opposite Half Acre Lane on the hillside at Blackrod.

A Roman road once connected Wigan with Manchester, passing through Westhoughton and Over Hulton and following roughly the route of the present A6 road. In 1757 part of another, narrower, Roman road was excavated at Blackrod, which appeared to follow a line towards another small Roman station at Mellor near Blackburn. The direction of this subsidiary road is described in 'Baines History of Lancashire' as follows: -

"It appears probable that this narrow road has run forward from Blackrode (Blackrod) by Street Fold and Water Street, near Rivington, and by White Hough in Tockholes, to the small Roman station at Blackburn, near the new road to Preston (i.e. Mellor)".

Views of Blackrod from a card postally used in 1907.

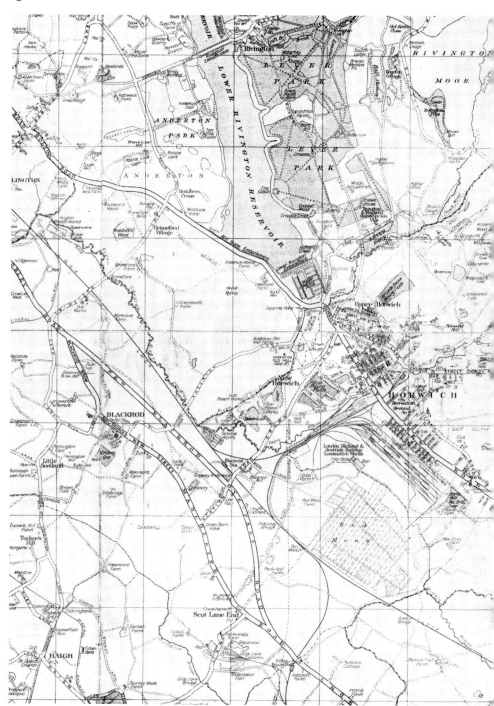

CHAPTER 3
The Forest of Horwich

The forest or 'chase' of Horwich was once situated within the Manor of Manchester and was owned by successive barons. It extended for six miles and was roughly sixteen miles in circumference. A forest or chase did not consist solely of dense woodland but also included open areas of grassland and heathland. Thomas Grelley, the sixth baron of Manchester, obtained the right of 'free warren' over the forest in 1294 and this entitled him to exclusive use of the lands. In order to monitor properly the movement of both people and animals in and out of the forest some form of boundary was essential and it is probable that the perimeter was fenced with hedges or paling, as was in fact the case with most other forests in the country.

Hunting game was a favourite pastime of the British Monarchy and the harsh 'Forest Laws' which were in force during Norman and Plantagenet times were principally designed to ensure that the Sovereign had an abundance of red deer to hunt. Three foresters or verderors were employed to look after the forest of Horwich and they were paid by landowners in Lostock, Rumworth, Heaton-under-the-forest, Longworth and Anderton. In addition to enforcing the Forest Laws, the foresters were responsible for the well being of the wild animals particularly the deer and hawks, collected the honey of the wild bees, often tended vaccaries (cattle pastures) on behalf of

the landowner, and were also expected to clear pathways through the brushwood to assist the hunting parties who regularly used the forest of Horwich. The following quote from Whittle's 'History of Bolton' (1855) refers to this period:-

> "This part (Horwich) was frequented by the barons bold of the county; knights and squires, yeoman and serfs, all joined in the chase, and the whole country rang with the noise of Norman beagles and the clang of horses' hoofs, through the vistas of wood and furze."

Any transgression against the Forest Laws was dealt with by the Court Baron or Court Leet which, due to the fact that Horwich was a sub-manor (that is the 'Upper Bailiwick' – forest in charge of a bailiff), sat within the confines of the forest and was known as a 'halmote'. The forest court was presided over by the lord of the sub-manor who could impose severe penalties including the gallows, the pit, the pillory and the tumbril.

Before a dog was allowed to enter the forest its feet had to pass through a metal stirrup or loop of a certain diameter. There is a curious case documented in the court records of the Lord of Manchester for 1254 concerning a dog. On a certain Saturday, Thomas, Grelley's bailiff was in the market-place at Manchester when he learned from men in the market that sometime previously they had heard dogs barking in the forest at Horwich. This information was sufficiently serious to warrant urgent investigation because the bailiff immediately set off for Horwich which was not an easy journey in those days. On his arrival he entered the forest and following a search he found a harrier (a dog used for hunting hares) belonging to Geoffrey de Chetham worrying the wild animals. As the record puts it, he did to that dog what seemed to him good. (A Short History of Manchester and Salford – F A Bruton – (1924).

The Greenwood Inn, Chorley New Road, Horwich. – Circa 1889. These appropriately titled premises were replaced by the present pub of the same name but stood on the opposite side of Chorley New Road quite some distance away.

An old legend exists concerning a particularly cruel and ruthless lord of the Manor of Horwich whose vindictiveness towards the foresters led to their having to take what justly belonged to them. The despotic lord then accused his foresters of lack of vigilance and summoned them to appear before his court. Knowing that they could not expect a fair trial the foresters concerned, along with a number of supporters, became 'outlaws' in the forest, seizing cattle and generally plundering and destroying forest preserves.

Eventually the leader of the 'outlaws' was captured and put to death. His body was left hanging from a tall oak tree while the flesh was picked from his bones by the eagles and other birds of prey.

Some little time after the 'lynching' the lord was called away from his home which abutted the forest and set off through the wood leaving his wife and three children unprotected. The lord's departure was witnessed by the 'outlaws' who seized the opportunity for revenge. They went to the manor house and abducted the three children from in front of their mother, slaughtered them and buried their small bodies near to where the bleached bones of their comrade still hung.

On the return of the manorial lord retribution was swift and the five persons responsible for the murder of those three innocents were themselves put to death. The site of the children's grave was not discovered and the spirits of the five desperadoes stalked the area in torment until the spot was finally exorcised by a 'worthy divine'!

'Robbers Walk' or 'Thieves Grave' which is associated with this old legend is situated on the pathway that once ran from Horwich, to Rivington and Blackrod Grammar School, across the old Horwich Race Course.

Horwich continued to be one complete Royal forest until the beginning of the

The Bee Hive Hotel, Chorley New Road, Horwich. – Circa 1880. This hotel was subsequently altered and extended. The name of the house is reminiscent of the time when Horwich was a complete Royal Forest and honey was a valuable commodity.

The Bee Hive Hotel. – Circa 1905.

The Squirrel Hotel, Scholes Bank, Horwich where the town initially grew as a bridge point settlement. The Squirrel Hotel can be seen in front of the leading motor coach.

The staff of the Bee Hive Hotel – Circa 1910.

The Squirrel Hotel is another public house, the name of which bears connection with the ancient forest.

Scholes Bank – 1908. The River Douglas runs under the road where the bridge parapet can be seen on the left.

17th Century although the claims of agriculture for land and the need of timber for both housing and fuel had greatly reduced the amount of woodland. The foresters were allowed to build wooden cottages or bothies in the forest and although Horwich was essentially a bridge point settlement it is quite possible that these rude dwellings were the nucleus of a part of the township.

Over the centuries Horwich has been variously spelt as Harewych, Horwiche, Horewych, etc., and the origin of the title remains in doubt. Two possibilities are that the name is derived from the Old English words 'haran wican' which simply mean grey wych elms or, alternatively, from 'haeran wic' meaning a 'village on stony ground'. Both explanations are possible in that the area was once covered by forest and is situated on the slopes of a Pennine spur, therefore it is a matter for individual choice which one is the more appropriate.

The Pennines are the source of many waterways which commence as fast flowing streams tumbling and cascading down the hillside before adopting a more sedate pace as they meander along the valleys and across the plains to the sea. The River Douglas, which means dark or black water, rises on Winter Hill flowing in a north westerly direction to the Ribble Estuary. Horwich, as a bridge point settlement, was initially developed from where the roadway crossed the River Douglas at a point near the Squirrel Hotel.

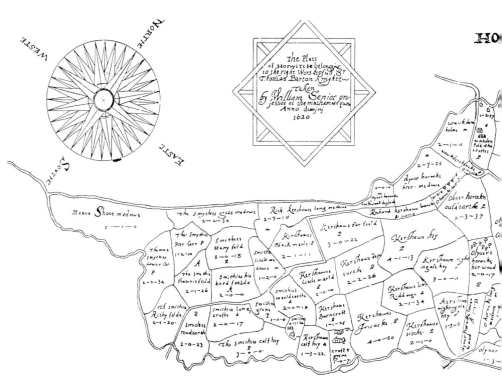

CHAPTER 4

The Platt of Horwich in 1620
(MAP AMENDED AFTER 1623)

Twenty years ago the earliest known map of Horwich came to light and was presented to the, then, Urban District Council by Councillor F R Yardley. This crudely drawn chart with its quaint inverted trees depicting water courses has proven to be of incalculable value as a link in the chain of local history. The map was commissioned in 1620 by Sir Thomas Barton and drawn by William Senior a professor of mathematics. It contains a detailed plan of Sir Thomas's holding in Horwich and includes the names of various tenants, the acreage of their respective tenancies and indicates any buildings which then existed. Along the top

of the map is shown the River Douglas. Purl Brook together with its various feeder streams provides the bottom boundary. Lee Lane disects the map in a diagonal, separating 'Olyver Horocks cowe hey' from 'Urmstons Lee' and 'Huntes cowe hey'. On the far left of the map where the waters join at 'Meane Shooe Medowe' is just north of Blackrod Railway Station. The right hand side of the map is bounded by the continuation of George's Lane leading to Rivington Pike. Top centre of the map in the corner of 'oerheuy greone' and next to 'Whittles brod-crofte' is the 'plague pit' where victims of the Great Plague of 1623 were buried.

17

CHAPTER 5
Farmstead Holdings

Some of the oldest buildings in Horwich are the farmsteads dotted about the hillside below the Pike. In the 16th and 17th centuries all the properties hereabouts had pathways connecting with the 'Old Hoghton Causey', an important thoroughfare which followed a high contour between Bolton and Hoghton Tower where, incidentally, James I of England knighted a loin of beef in 1617, resulting in the expression 'Sir-Loin'.

Each and every one of these farmstead holdings has a unique and interesting past deserving of special mention but available space and time prevent this. A random selection is however included which I am sure will reflect the richness of Horwich's agricultural heritage.

Hodgkinson Fold Farm, Wilderswood, Horwich

Hodgkinson Fold Farm dates from Elizabethan times and is one of Horwich's oldest farmstead dwellings. It was once surrounded by four small cottages and a barn.

The Trades Directory of 1902 shows George Sinker farming Hodgkinson Fold and Giles Meadow. The Sinker family were brickmakers who moved to Horwich from Crewe when Horwich Locomotive Works was scheduled to be built. After their completion George Sinker secured employment carting for Albert Cotton Mill before commencing a

18

successful dairy farming business for which he is perhaps best remembered.

Hodgkinson Fold Farm – Circa 1900 – The girl in the photograph is Florence Kay. In the wall to her left is a post box.

Ormston's Farm, Wilderswood, Horwich

Ormston's Farm was the result of a feoffment (mode of conveying freehold estate by formal transfer of possession) in 1513 between John Barton and Richard Urmston in recompense for the latter's true, diligent and faithful service to the former. The gift also enabled Richard's son James to pursue his studies at St John's College Cambridge where he obtained a Fellowship in 1523.

In 1574 Robert Barton of Smithills granted a 301 year lease for the same tenement to Roger Urmston thus ensuring continued occupation for the family. This security of tenure was jeopardised in 1625 when Roger's son, Richard, was 'outlawed' for stealing two sheep. But it does not seem that they were dispossessed because ten years later Margaret, the widow first of Roger Urmston then Thomas Anderton, assigned the lease for the benefit of her three children Margaret, Jane and John.

Sir Thomas Barton, a descendant of John Barton the original feoffer, reclaimed the property in 1637 and eventually sold it back to Francis Anderton in 1652. For many years the manorial rights and estate of Horwich were owned by the Anderton family. By Robert Blundell's will dated 24th July 1809 the estate passed to his two daughters Catherine – wife of Thomas Stoner, and Elizabeth – wife of Stephen Tempest.

The property eventually passed to the Wright family who owned it until the late 1800's. The Reverend Henry Wright is recorded as a lessor to successive tenants. The last person to actually farm the estate was Richard Owen.

Ormston's Farm 1920

Foxholes House, Foxholes, Horwich

For over a century Foxholes House was the home of the Mason family who farmed the area where Foxholes and Stoneycroft Estates now stand.

Mrs Mason was a descendant of the Lords Willoughby-de-Parham who were extensive landowners in Horwich and Rivington during the 17th and 18th centuries. Before moving to 'Shaw Place', Anderton, the manorial seat was situated near to the old Horwich Race Course. It is thought that the name 'Old Lords' is derived from this connection. Four noble Lords of the lineage are buried in Horwich Parish Churchyard.

Foxholes House – 1910

Stone quarried for the building of the last Horwich Chapel was used to build Foxholes Cottages in 1832. The prop-erties were owned by the Mason family and originally tenanted by their em-ployees.

Foxholes Cottages – 1920

Although widowed in 1854, Mrs Mason continued to work the farm with her three daughters Elizabeth, Mary and Anne. The sisters were skilled at all tasks around the farm, including thatching, haymaking and general repair work. None of them ever married and despite their wealth chose to live a relatively frugal existence. They were very shrewd business women and extremely beneficent, particularly in relation to local Methodism, contributing largely to the erection of the Mason Memorial Chapel on Lee Lane.

One by one the family died out, the girls' mother died in 1863, followed by Elizabeth and then Mary. It is reported that up to her death in 1903 Anne refused to buy new clothes for herself, choosing instead to wear up those belonging to her sisters.

In 1901 Horwich Council was allowed to construct a water reservoir on land belonging to the Mason family at Markland's Farm. Anne Mason attached a condition to the permission that no water rates should be levied on either Foxholes House or the cottages. On Anne's demise two years later, the gross amount of her estate totalled a staggering £22,828.

Agreement for the building of Marklands Reservoir.

Foxholes House was converted from a farm house to a private residence in 1900 and one of the cottages (extreme right in photograph) became the farmer's home.

Manor House, Wilderswood, Horwich

In 1620 the Manor House site belonged to the Hunt family who owned a tract of land between Lee Lane and George's Lane in what is now the Brownlow Road area. The Horrocks family occupied adjoining land and there seems to have been a good neighbourly spirit as in 1699 the two families were sharing eleven seats at the Parish Church. Eventually the Horrockses took over Hunt's estate. The development of Rockhaven from 1840 by Richard Brownlow, son of Christopher Brownlow of Manor House, consolidated the holdings of this Rivington family in the area.

Manor House, Wilderswood – 1984

Higher Meadows Farm, Wilderswood, Horwich

This farm is situated near to the Wilderswood Stream and was known locally as Rothwells, most probably due to the practice of perpetuating the name of a well known tenant long after their death.

The property was once used as a weekend home by Thomas Offord who had a plumbing business in Horwich and Adlington. Higher Meadows Farm was eventually demolished by Blackrod Council, the last tenant being Harry Hoyle who had a hardware shop in Winter Hey Lane.

Higher Meadows Farm – Circa 1900.

Higher Meadows Farm during the summer – Circa 1905. The last load of hay being taken back to Higher Meadows Farm. It obviously took two horses to draw the loaded haycart up the hillside. One can sympathise with the ladies who must have been pretty hot and uncomfortable particularly wearing such fine millinery.

Higher Meadows Farm during the winter – Circa 1910.

Higher Meadows Farm was once used as a weekend home by local plumber and glazier Thomas Offord, whose business advert is shown here.

Harper's Farm, Wilderswood, Horwich

Harper's Farm was last used for agricultural purposes by the Ison family who are still represented in the area.

The farmhouse eventually became a waterman's cottage and prior to the Second World War was occupied by Sam Hamer and family who had responsibility for supervising the water catchment area

Harper's Farm – Circa 1900 – The children shown in the photograph have obviously been interrupted while at play although curiosity about the cameraman seems to have kept their attention.

Harper's Farm 1930 – Rockhaven Castle can be seen in the background. (Sam Hamer is pushing the wheelbarrow).

on behalf of Blackrod Council. Ramblers could visit the cottage and obtain light refreshments at modest prices. The gar-

den areas were always well tended and it must have been a pleasant spot to rest a while.

Slack Farm, Horwich Moor – Circa 1890. This scene typifies farm life in the area during the late 19th century. The Thompson family shown in the photograph later leased Wilderswood Farm.

Wilderswood Farm, Wilderswood, Horwich – Circa 1920. Mr S Thompson of Wilderswood Farm delivering milk in the area.

Dickinson's Farm, Horwich – Circa 1904. Hilton Estate was developed where this farm once stood.

Mason Fold Farm, Horwich – Circa 1961.

Chapel-in-the Fields Poultry Farm, Horwich

Claypool Estate has since been built on the extensive acres of Mr H Whalley's poultry farm. The crescent of houses on the left of the photograph included Brazley Avenue.

Chapel-in-the-Fields is derived from New Chapel, once encircled by fields and farms, which on the weekday has always looked down on more cows than christians. (History of New Chapel, Horwich – Francis George Collier – 1877).

Chapel-in-the-Fields Poultry Farm, Horwich – Circa 1935.

Dulson's Farm, Bolton Fold, Horwich – 1961.

Sefton Fold Farm, Horwich – 1961.

Detail of Date Stone over doorway of Sefton Fold Farm.

CHAPTER 6
Spinners and Weavers

Henry VIII's historian, Leland, visited Lancashire in 1538 and commented in his Itinerary – "Divers villages in the Mores (Moors) about Bolton do make cottons". However, raw cotton was not brought into England until the end of the sixteenth century, over fifty years after Leland's death, and it seems that he was in fact referring to 'woollens'.

When raw cotton was eventually introduced into England the main woollen centres of East Anglia and the West Country refused to adopt it, chiefly because the rich woollen-merchants had a vested interest in resisting change. Lancashire was free from any such restriction and readily accepted the challenge which the manufacture of cotton cloth offered. The county has a heavy annual rainfall, principally due to the prevailing winds, moisture laden owing to the warm Gulf Stream, hitting cold air as they rise on meeting the Pennines. Moist air makes cotton fibre soft and easy to handle and thus ideal climatic conditions existed for cotton production.

Initially, cotton was used solely for 'weft' (the fibre running across the width of a bolt of cloth) because no one could spin cotton yarn of sufficient strength to make 'warp' (the fibre running lengthwise) having, instead, to use wool or more often linen. Material produced in this manner was known as fustian. The ability to weave pure cotton cloth did however eventually develop.

There are four principal processes involved in the manufacture of cottons. They are 'carding' – combing the cotton fibres, 'spinning' – twisting the fibres together to make them strong enough for the warp and weft, 'weaving' – interlacing the warp and weft, and 'finishing' – bleaching, dyeing or printing patterns on the finished cloth.

By 1750 the cotton industry had become the chief employment of the people of South Lancashire. In Horwich, as in many other towns and villages, landowners organised the supply of raw materials for producing cotton cloth and put them out to their tenants or local residents to be carded, spun and woven. They would then buy back the cloth and re-sell it to merchants who took it away on packhorses for dyeing before trading it commercially in the principal towns and cities.

As the demand for cotton goods grew, more and more people became involved in their production until there was barely a single house in Horwich which did not possess either a handloom or a spinning wheel, or both. Agriculture was still important because the village, as it then was, remained largely self supporting, producing its own food, making its own clothes and agricultural implements and brewing its own beer. Many of those producing cotton also worked in the fields for a part of the year.

30

Horwich still boasts a number of weavers, cottages but their often smart appearance belies any connection with the 'cottage industry' which grew up around textiles.

Club Houses, Church Street, Horwich – 1915.

The Club Houses are shown on the left of this photograph with steps at the front. In the early 1800's handloom weaving was carried out in the cellars of these cottages and the residents supplemented their diet by keeping pigs and poultry in the wide back street.

Brinks Row Cottages – 1900.

Handloom weaving was once carried out in these stone cottages and the woven articles were sold to the Rothwell family who lived at Grut Farm in Rivington. The cottage on the extreme left was the home of Mr Finch the one time owner of Pilkington Delph on Horwich Moor. Stone quarried from here was used to provide foundations for mill engines at several Bolton factories.

The name 'Brinks Row' was carved in a stone, set into the outside wall of one of these cottages. During recent building alterations the stone nameplate was removed revealing the date 1759 on the reverse. This is believed to be the year in which the premises were built.

In addition to weavers, the cottages have also housed colliers and quarrymen over the years. Various landlords have included Andrew Peak who was a brickmaker of some note and Lord Leverhulme.

Bottom O'th Moor, Chorley Old Road, Horwich – 1920.
These rows of Stone Cottages built in the late eighteenth century were originally occupied by handloom weavers. The local partnership of Greenhalgh and Bispham who traded as 'putters out of yarn' supplied the raw material to the weavers and purchased back the finished cloth. Among these dwellings were two beerhouses known as 'Plumptons' and 'The Mason's Arms' respectively.

Close-up view of Bolton O'th Moor Cottages – 1909.

The erection of the weaving shed at Victoria Mill, Chorley New Road, Horwich.

Carnival Float for Telford Mill – Circa 1920.

Handloom Weavers Cottages 200, 202 & 204 Lee Lane, Horwich. The weaving rooms were in the loft. Premises demolished in 1967.

Weavers' Cottages, Lee Lane, Horwich.

Stone built in the second storey of the centre cottage of the block numbered 192, 194 and 196 Lee Lane, Horwich.

Stone built in the second storey of the centre cottage of the block numbered 200, 202 and 204, Lee Lane, Horwich.

Drawings of Date Stones from demolished weavers' cottages (drawn by John Rawlinson).

CHAPTER 7
The Crofters

Mrs Kay's Croft, Wilderswood, Horwich – 1900. The building shown at the front centre is known as Mrs Kay's Croft from its connection with 'atmospheric' bleaching. Brinks Row Cottages can be seen in the middle distance with Rockhaven Castle standing on the horizon.

Prior to the introduction of chemical bleaching in 1790, woven cottons, fustians and other fabrics were 'whitened' by repeated boilings in alkaline solutions or buttermilk and exposure to the suns rays. 'Atmospheric' bleaching, or 'grassing' was an extremely slow process which took several weeks to complete.

Copious amounts of water were required for 'grassing' and streams flowing from the hills around Bolton meant that the area was ideally suited for this textile finishing process.

It was a capital offence to break into a bleachcroft and steal cloth but despite this thefts were relatively common. In August 1798, John Eccles appeared at Lancaster Assizes for stealing calico belonging to Messrs Tipping from a bleachcroft in Horwich Vale, and a similar offence against Mr Entwistle of Rivington. He was sentenced to death and prior to his execution is said to have acknowledged the justice of his sentence.

The names of many old bleaching families are perpetuated in the areas they once owned and used for crofting. 'Hopwood Hill' derives its name from the Hopwood family who are included in a list of Manchester merchants of 1788; and 'Grundy Hill', which lies between Church Street and Chorley New Road and where Horwich Football Club now plays, is similarly derived.

Crofting is inextricably linked with agriculture, spinning and weaving in that a household could be involved in all these activities, possibly using an infertile piece of land as a beachcroft to enhance its value.

Many of the old cottages once involved in textile manufacture have disappeared while others leave no clue as to their past. Tottering Temple was a small bleachworks which stood on Scholes Bank and was demolished during road widening. The Old Original Bay Horse public house in Lee Lane was also a bleacher's home.

Before the A673 road was built, Scholes Bank stood on a high rise overlooking Horwich Vale. The black-scowling appearance of this promontory caused it to be named 'Scowl Bank' which was later corrupted to 'Scholes Bank'. On entering Horwich from Anderton the dual carriageway which is now Scholes Bank is so impressive that it bespeaks a town of much greater proportions.

Illustrations are included to show the widening of Scholes Bank and various properties once connected with bleaching.

Scholes Bank – 1903. A view taken from Lee Lane.

Scholes Bank – Circa 1946. This view was taken before the road was widened. Tottering Temple is the building on the extreme right.

Scholes Bank - Circa 1946. The cottages on the right lost garden area when the road was widened.

Scholes Bank – Circa 1950. Tottering Temple has disappeared with the construction of the dual carriageway.

Crofter's Arms – Circa 1890. The origin of the pub's name is clearly connected with open air bleaching. This row of terraced cottages including the pub was known locally as 'Tup Row' (Top Row). It was demolished in the 1930's.

'Ye Jolly Crofters' which replaced the 'Crofter's Arms'.

Before the steam engine came into use generally, the textile industry was entirely dependent upon a good supply of running water, hence the reason for many premises connected with textile manufacture being situated near to rivers and streams. The River Douglas, Wilderswood Stream and Purl Brook once supported Horwich's operations. Indeed, the Wilderswood Stream had a small factory every few hundred yards along its length.

'Swallowfield', Lower Brazley, Horwich – Circa 1920. Home of the Ingham family who were prominent in the local bleaching industry.

Top O'th Such Horwich – 1920. These cottages built about 1801 were initially occupied by crofters connected with the Ridgway family's bleaching business. The road running in front of the dwellings led to Wallsuches Bleachworks, hence the name 'Top O'th Such'. At the beginning of this century allotments situated opposite the cottages were being used by the tenants. One of the dwellings was also used as a grocery and provisions shop.

Star Bleachworks – Horwich Vale – Circa 1930.

Workers leaving the Star Bleachworks – 1904.

CHAPTER 8
The Ridgway Family

In 1770, two brothers, John and Thomas Ridgway, owned bleachcrofts at either side of the River Croal in Bolton. The site was originally known as 'Dog Brow' until a pair of gates were erected at the entrance to deter thieves, when it became 'Ridgway Gates'.

A fire in 1775 destroyed much of the Ridgway's stock-in-trade and led to a re-think of business policy. The increasing demand for cotton cloth gave scope for expansion and prompted the brothers to look around for a larger site. Several properties were surveyed including Wallsuches at Horwich, which eventually proved to be the most suitable. The first lease of Wallsuches was taken out in 1777 for a period of 99 years. Henry Blundell was the lessor.

Although Wallsuches was leased jointly to John and Thomas Ridgway, it does not appear that John ever became directly involved in setting up bleaching operations. In fact he continued to trade under his own name in Bolton and, until his death on the 2nd November 1800, lived at Chamber Hall, Bolton. Perhaps John's ties with Bolton were too strong to break. He was familiar with the town and enjoyed local standing there. As a trus-

Lee Lane, Horwich – 1900.

Lee Lane, Horwich – Circa 1916.

tcc of Bolton Grammar School he is credited with playing an important part in the election of one of its most distinguished masters, John Lempriere (1765 – 1824) notable for his 'Classical Dictionary'.

'Dog Brow' was eventually sold to Bolton Corporation for £800 and, incidentally, the Market hall now stands on the spot.

When Thomas Ridgway first moved his bleaching operations into Horwich the place was little more than a village and, judging by the description in Hampson's History of Horwich, a very drab place as well:-

"The roads were wretched and uncared for; property was a commodity of little value. Only the few houses which even to-day (1883) bear their ancient names relieved the bleak and cheerless surroundings; no distinguishing mark to break the monotony; the moorland, with its heather covered

background, and rocky cliffs gave a barren aspect to the landscape".

"Lee Lane was a narrow, undignified thoroughfare, with some three or four houses at considerable distance from each other".

Wallsuches Bleachworks

By 1780 the single hut-like structure which had stood on the Wallsuches site before Thomas Ridgway arrived was replaced with a bleachworks requiring six water wheels to drive its machinery.

Employment was provided at Wallsuches not only for the people of Horwich but for those from neighbouring Blackrod, Rivington and Adlington, many of whom moved into Horwich to live. As the business expanded, Thomas Ridgway took his son Joseph into the concern on the latter's twenty first birthday in 1786. Some time later a second son, named Thomas after his father, was allowed into the partnership, which then traded as Thomas Ridgway and Sons. Success brought prosperity not only to the Ridgways but to their workforce. It was a 'boom-time' when people had money to spend but a changing social

Wallsuches Bleachworks – Circa 1933. This photograph was taken about the time that Wallsuches closed as a bleachworks in 1933. The building on the extreme left was the Engine House the pride of the works. Standing behind the chimney is St George's Bleachcroft a five storey building, 30 bays long, which was known locally as 'Gingham House'. No 1 Bleachcroft is shown extreme right.

order creates its own special needs and it is to the eternal credit of the Ridgway family that they recognised this and did something about it.

Horwich Parish Church School

Education was seriously lacking in Horwich in those days and there were no schools in existence. The only formal teaching available was from an old dame who had seen better days. She taught the basic alphabet in what passed for a school.

The Ridgways realised the need for a school but were astute enough to appreciate that if the suggestion first came from them, the workers might well oppose the idea, particularly as very young children were wage earners and their income would be lost. In order to overcome this, the workers were initially encouraged to improve their own learning and in due course sufficient in-

Horwich Parish Church School.

A class of girl pupils at Horwich Parish Church School – 1890.

terest had been generated for the work-force to propose that a schoolhouse was built. A subscription fund was then orga-nised and in 1793 the first school in Horwich was opened at the east end of the church.

For many years the accounts of the church and the school were administered together. Ralph Howarth was one of the earliest masters who had between 75 and 100 pupils in his charge. His tasks included cleaning the school, lighting fires for heating, and buying all the text books and stationery from Wigan. For these onerous duties his salary was £2.10s 0d. (£2.50) per quarter and 2s.0d (10 pence) per journey to Wigan, which was paid from collections taken at the Sunday School Sermons.

Horwich Parish Church – (the second building)

The Holy Trinity Parish Church is at least the third one to be built on the present site. In 1565 the Commission-ers for Removing Superstitious Orna-ments took vestment, albe, altar cloth, corpasse and other idolatrous gear from Horwich Chapel. It is recorded that the first chapel was erected by a local tailor who was paid 2d (less than one pence) per day for his labours. He agreed to complete the commission provided that he could incorporate an emblem of his trade in the structure and to this end a large pair of scissors was sculptured in a key-stone. With the advent of Wallsuches Bleachworks the population of Horwich grew fairly rapidly and in 1782 this original church was replaced by a larger one.

A copy by Mr Rawlinson of an original drawing of the old chapel which was replaced in 1831 by the present Holy Trinity Parish Church.

The 'Stocks' and the 'White House'.

About the end of the eighteenth century the Pilkington family was prominent in Horwich and owned both the 'Stocks' and the 'White House'. Thomas Ridgway initially rented the 'Stocks' from the Pilkingtons in 1787 but eventually bought both properties.

The 'Stocks' derived its name from the fact that the village stocks, in which

The 'Stocks' – Circa 1910.

View of the 'Stocks' from Fleet Street – 1910.

Chorley Old Road, Horwich – 1930. A view of Chorley Old Road looking up hill towards Bolton. The semi-detached houses on the right replaced the 'Stocks' which was demolished in 1911.

wrong-doers were once clamped as a punishment, stood nearby. This penalty was last used locally in 1805. Richard Pilkington lived at the 'Stocks' from 1761 to 1796. The property was situated on the Stocks Estate which adjoined the Pilkington Estate where the 'White House' stood. In the early period of his tenancy the 'Stocks' was one of a number of small cottages situated in a fold. The road from Horwich to Bolton originally ran past the 'Stocks', up Fleet Street, across the front of the 'White House' and out onto Higher Barn and Top Row. In 1763 the Bolton and Nightingale Trust was set up under the Turnpike Trusts Act to improve the road system and the original road was diverted with the result that it cut through the 'Stocks' fold and divided it. Stocks Estate passed into the hands of the Ridgways in 1803.

Richard Pilkington lived at the 'White House' until his death in 1786 at the advanced age of 93 years. Ridgmont House was developed on the site of the 'White House' when the Ridgway family purchased the Pilkington Estate in 1801.

Horwich Building Club

A Building Society existed in Horwich as early as 1802 when the Ridgways appointed a committee to run their 'Building Club'. Portions of the 'Stocks Estate' were offered on long leases with easy repayments so that Wallsuches employees could build and own their own houses. The Club ceased to exist in 1822.

Thomas Ridgway

Thomas Ridgway, who had been the instrument of so much achievement

Ridgmont House – Circa 1900.

Gatehouse to Rigmont House – 1930. The Jolly Crofters pub can be seen standing behind.

locally, died at Southport on the 30th August 1816 aged 77 years. He is described in Hampson's History of Horwich as:-

"distinguished for his unostentatious demeanour; his character was exemplified in that energy which not only manifested itself in the success which attended his mercantile efforts, but also in the still greater development, a prosperous village".

The second generation of the Ridgways

By his will, dated 16th April 1814, Thomas Ridgway left his holdings to be shared equally between his two sons Joseph and Thomas (Jnr). Because there were no specific details of what each brother should receive a dispute ensued. This was only resolved when John Ashworth of Turton agreed to act as an independent arbitrator. In the event, all the land to the north side of Chorley Old Road went to Thomas and that on the south side to Joseph. In addition, the latter was to have all the timber on the estate.

The motto of the Ridgway family crest was compiled by a Horwich schoolmaster who received twenty guineas from Thomas Ridgway (Jnr) for using an anagram of the latter's name to construct it. "Mihi gravato Deus" was the result, which although it does not contain all the letters was nevertheless considered suitable. A translation of the Ridgway motto is "God is with me when I am weighed down".

Joseph Ridgway became well known for his hunting exploits. He is said to have possessed thirty of the finest harriers ever seen whose only fault was that they were too much of a match for the hare. He became a local magistrate and was honoured with the appointment as Deputy Lieutenant of Lancashire.

Despite being lamed in an accident, Thomas Ridgway was equally active. His interest lay in 'coursing', as opposed to

Sable, 2 wings conjoined or.

The Ridgway Family Crest.

'hunting', and cattle breeding. In 1834 he was elected president of the Bolton Cattle Fair Society.

Prior to the introduction of police forces as we understand them today, the office of 'constable' was an honorary post, usually held by a local dignitary who generally delegated the duties to a deputy. Thomas Ridgway was the last person to hold this office in Horwich.

'Thomas Ridgway and Sons' has been described as one of the most enterprising bleaching firms of the time. Although founded in 1777 in the days of 'atmospheric' bleaching the most successful period for the works came with the advent of 'chlorine' bleaching. Two local bleaching families, the Ridgways and the Ainsworths of Moss Bank, Bolton, sponsored the efforts of Matthew Vallet, a French chemist, in this direction. When introduced, chemical bleaching reduced the time needed for the process from several weeks to a few hours. 'Gingham House' a five storey bleaching mill erected at Wallsuches was the first factory of the Industrial Revolution to come to Horwich. Watt's steam engine replaced the water-driven mill wheels in 1798 and the first 'glazing callender' – which gives a glazed finish to cloth by applying heated irons – was erected there.

In the late eighteenth century other bleachworks and calico print mills were established in the area. On the Horwich and Rivington boundary at Shaw Brook in the Douglas Valley a second bleachworks was set up where a 'glazing calender' and steam power were also used.

Horwich

Bleachworks

The site of Horwich Bleachworks was once owned by the Hopwood family and was bought by Richard Pilkington who lived at the 'Stocks'. When the Ridgways bought the lease for Stocks Estate in 1803 the bleachworks was included. However, on the 31st May 1820, Horwich Bleachworks was purchased from the Ridgways by Messrs France and Pass and, in October 1840, it again changed hands when William (Squire) Longworth secured the property. Longworth was involved in several local business concerns notably the colliery industry. He was proprietor at Doffcocker, Westhoughton and Brinsop Hall pits. Squire Longworth died on the 16th September 1861, aged 65 years and the works were inherited by his only surviving son who then lived at 'The Knowles'.

Horwich Parish Church (the third building).

In 1774, prior to the arrival of the Ridgways in Horwich, the population was 305 – comprising 156 females and 149 males. By 1801 it had risen to 1,565 and by 1831 this figure had more than doubled to 3,562. The existing church was inadequate to accommodate the potential congregation represented by this increase and a new and larger place of worship was a necessity. Fate took a hand in the shape of the King's Commissioners for building New Churches who were authorised to allocate £1 million for this purpose. The money was made available to celebrate the English victory against the French in the Napoleonic Wars. Horwich received a portion of this money which was supplemented by subscriptions from the principal inhabitants of the town, notably the Ridgways.

On Friday 21st May 1830, Joseph Ridgway laid the foundation stone for the new church then placed a bottle containing coins in a prepared cavity. Following the ceremony the dignitaries present were provided with a meal at either Ridgmont House or one of the hostelries in Horwich. A sizeable contribution was made by the Ridgways to the new building and in recognition of their generosity the family crest was included in the church tower. When completed the Holy Trinity Parish Church had seating for 1,500 persons and the beauty of its gothic architecture can still be seen.

Horwich Parish Church, Church Street, Horwich – 1911. The new chancel on the right was erected in 1901 in memory of the Reverend H S Pigot, MA.

The Ridgway Crest on Horwich Parish Church.

The Reverend David Hewitt succeeded Reverend Samuel Johnson as incumbent at Horwich Parish Church in 1826 and officiated at the foundation stone laying ceremony and subsequent opening of the church for religious worship. It seems that Joseph Ridgway had a difference of opinion with Reverend Hewitt when the latter would not allow him to walk in a church procession because he did not hold office at the church. A bitter feud developed between the two men with allegations and counter allegations. Reverend Hewitt often complained of noisy parties at Ridgmont House. This resulted in Joseph Ridgway erecting a mound on his estate, ostensibly to commemorate the death of one of his racehorses named General Jeffrey. A statue of this horse was in fact placed on top of the mound. The prominence was intended as a 'hill of spite' to block Reverend Hewitt's view of Ridgmont House from the vicarage. The hill is now known as 'daffodil hill'. Drunken revellers destroyed the statue in 1859.

The house on the left was once the Vicarage where Reverend David Hewitt lived.

'Daffodil Hill' – 'The Hill of Spite'.

Interior, Horwich Parish Church.

Joseph Ridgway died on the 26th June 1842, never having reconciled his differences with Reverend Hewitt. All the bequests in Joseph's will for the benefit of Horwich Parish Church were suspended until Reverend Hewitt left the parish. He eventually resigned in 1852 and was succeeded by the Reverend Pigot. One condition of Joseph Ridgway's will was that he was buried in the family vault and the executors were directed to erect a monument to his memory in Horwich Parish Church costing not less than £1,000. The result is the beautiful Westmacott Statue which is a lifelike figure of Mrs Ridgway at prayer, sculptured in white marble.

The Third Generation of the Ridgways

Although Joseph Ridgway married twice he died without issue and the Ridgway line was continued through his brother Thomas (Jnr). The latter married Miss Gill of Bolton who bore him two sons, Thomas and Joseph. Thomas, the elder son, was killed tragically in a

The 'Friends of Wallsuches' – Circa 1908. This group of women, known as the 'Friends of Wallsuches' was in service at Wallsuches House, the home of the bleachworks owner, which stands in its own grounds quite close to the factory. The lady standing back centre is Mrs Partington whose son Jim wrote 'The two-up and two-downer' – an autobiography which includes reference to his early life in Horwich.

hunting accident at Euxton, near Chorley, when he was still quite young. 'Young Joe', as he was affectionately known, continued to run the family business displaying many of the admirable qualities of his forebears.

The young Joseph first married Selina Harriet and the couple had a son, Thomas Hastings Ridgway, and a daughter, Cecily. Acting on doctor's advice, Joseph together with his wife and young son went to spend the winter of 1860 in the warm climate of Egypt. While at Thebes, Joseph became very ill and his wife stoically nursed him until help could be summoned via an English clergyman in Cairo. Tragically, Mrs Ridgway became infected with her husband's illness and she died in Egypt. Joseph eventually recovered but his young son was so weakened by the experience that he too died at the early age of seventeen. Cecily, incidentally, married the Honorable J Stuart Hardy.

On his return to Wallsuches, following the tragedy in Egypt, Joseph married his second wife, the sister of Lord Colville. He later left the district to live in Kent. His death occurred at Eaton Place, London, on the 20th January 1879 when he was 59 years old.

Subsequent Ownership of Wallsuches.

In 1818 Thomas (Jnr.) and Joseph Ridgway brought their 23 year old nephew, Thomas Ridgway Bridson, into the partnership. He left in 1834 to set up in business on his own account. Another partnership then ensued involving two long standing employees, Charles and Christopher Howarth, who subsequently became sole owners. Joseph Howarth, a descendant of the same family, eventually sold Wallsuches to the Bleachers Association in 1900.

'Moor Platt' – Circa 1890. A group photograph taken in front of 'Moor Platt'.

'Wallsuches House' and 'Moor Platt'.

During their period of tenure at Wallsuches the Howarth family lived at 'Wallsuches House' which is situated within the factory confines and at 'Moor Platt' which was sadly destroyed by fire.

The closûre of Wallsuches bleachworks in 1933 marked the end of an era but the Ridgway family's association with Horwich will always be remembered.

Redundancy notice for a Wallsuches employee – 1933.

Moor Platt – Horwich.

Close-up view of the Black Bull – Circa 1910.

View across Ridgmont Cemetery – Circa 1925.

'The Stocks' Cottage, Fleet Street, Horwich – 1903.

CHAPTER 9
Water Mills

As industry became more mechanised towards the end of the eighteenth century it was no longer economically possible to sustain the 'cottage industry'. The first moves towards industrialisation were made by enlarging existing dwellings, sometimes knocking two cottages into one, so that machinery could be housed. Gradually, small factories were purpose built for the manufacture and finishing of textiles. To refer to these early centres of spinning, weaving

Crowther Fold Mill – 1920. The pear tree behind Mr Kitchen was planted by Joseph Crowther in the late 18th century. It has since been removed because the roots damaged the foundations.

Crowther Fold Mill (front view) – 1950. At the time this photograph was taken the mill buildings were in a derelict state although they have since been renovated. The mill can be seen on the right with the mill owners house on the left.

and finishing as factories is a misnomer because, in effect, they were only slightly larger than dwelling houses. Nevertheless, labour was employed and work was organised so that the only difference between them and their more modern counterparts was a distinct lack of facilities for the workers.

Crowther Fold Mill

Crowther Fold Mill is probably the oldest spinning mill in Horwich and some say that it was the birthplace of cotton manufacture in Lancashire. It is situated by the side of the Wilderswood Steam where an old bleachcroft was once operated known as Hunte's White Croft.

The partnership of Crowther and Wingfield owned Crowther Fold Mill and employed a number of children from the Standish Workhouse among the workforce. Power was provided by a water wheel. In order to ensure a constant supply of water for the wheel a series of mill lodges were constructed.

The mill was consecrated to hold religious services for local Methodists who, until 1810 when the first chapel was built in Chapel Street, had no place of worship in Horwich. Every Sunday, Mr William Thornley walked from his home in Bolton to preach at Crowther Fold Mill. Much effort was spent in preparing the mill for his arrival.

Crowther Fold Mill (rear view) – 1950. The waterwheel which was installed behind the mill owners house (shown on the right) has been removed but it is easy to imagine it revolving slowly and sedately in those bygone days.

Gorton Fold – Circa 1830. Gorton Fold was built in 1714 and this view is taken from a painting dated about 1830. The Mill is seen here on the left. To the right is a barn and the workers' cottages are situated in the centre. The cottages still exist and are occupied to this day.

Gorton Fold Mill, Horwich

Gorton Fold Mill dates from 1714 and also lays claim to being the birthplace of the cotton trade. It was originally connected with the bleaching industry and the crofts stretched away behind the mill as far as Chorley New Road. Purl Brook drove the water wheel which powered machinery at the mill. In 1851 the owner of Gorton House was William Bennett whose nephew Richard Bennett was the proprietor of Wilderswood Mill.

At a time when Horwich Parish Church was one of only a few established places of worship in Horwich, several denomi-nations including the Catholics, Unitarians and Methodists held religious services at Gorton Fold. A rota was drawn up to achieve equitable use of the accommodation provided.

Mill Hole Cottage, Wilderswood, Horwich.

Mill Hole Cottage was once a textile mill with its own lodge supplied by the Wilderswood Stream. It has had a variety of names and uses over the years. In 1804 an agreement between John Hopwood and Richard Pilkington

Gorton Cottage, Lee Lane, Horwich – Circa 1880. The proprietor of Foxholes Mill lived at Gorton Cottage.

Gorton Cotttage - 1909.

Mill Hole Cottage – Circa 1880. An exceptionally pleasing study of life in Horwich when both farming and textile manufacture were run from these premises. Standing to the left are Factory Hill cottages which were demolished in 1939. The roadway in the foreground is listed as the 'Old Highway' and led to Mill Lane. From behind where the children are seated a pathway followed the boundary wall and eventually connected with the top of Brownlow Road.

refers to the latter reserving his carding place, access and water rights at 'Mill Holl'. Teasels still grow in the garden at Mill Hole. This plant is similar to a thistle and for hundreds of years the hooked hairs on the seed heads were used to 'tease' up the fibres on woollen cloth. Their main use today, incidentally, is to pull up the nap on the green baize covering of snooker tables.

Mill Hole Cottage – Circa 1940. A later view of Mill Hole Cottage, from a post card issued by H G Hutchinson of Horwich. The outbuildings have disappeared and Factory Hill Cottages are no longer visible, which suggests that the photograph was taken after 1939.

Well Cottage, Wilderswood, Horwich

Well Cottage was originally called Wilderswood Springs and according to the 1851 Census it was then occupied by Thomas Folds Heaton, aged 24 years, his wife Catherine, aged 22 years, and their three children. The family also had a thirteen year old girl whom they employed as a house servant. A rating valuation of £51.9s.8d. levied on the property in 1850 included reference to '15 Horse Steam Power' and a 'Drying Cylinder House'.

Wilderswood Mill, Wilderswood, Horwich

The partnership of Crowther and Wingfield who operated Crowther Fold Mill are believed to have developed Wilderswood Mill to service an expanding business. They sold out their interest in the Mill in the early 1800's to Mr Wylde and his son William. Samuel Crompton, inventor of the 'Spinning Mule', was at one time involved with the concern.

Henry Stones, a talented Horwich engineer who worked at Wilderswood

Mill, had an acquaintanceship with Crompton which proved fortuitous for the latter. Stones suggested to Crompton that in order to improve the reliability of his 'Mule' he should replace the crude wooden rollers with fluted metal ones. On adopting this suggestion the 'Mule' proved to be much more commercially viable. A number of these 'improved Mules' were eventually installed at Wilderswood Mill.

In due course Mr Wylde's son-in-law, Richard Bennett, took over the busi-ness. The 1851 Census mentions Richard Bennett as proprietor of Wilderswood Mill with 127 workers on the payroll. In 1857 the mill changed hands again and was successively managed, first by Mr W Greenhalgh and then by his son Thomas Bancroft Greenhalgh, until its closure in 1898. The Mill was finally demolished in 1911. An example of the 'Mule' was taken from Wilderswood Mill and was preserved for a time in the Chadwick Museum in Bolton Park. Following the closure of this museum, the 'Mule' was transferred elsewhere.

Well Cottage – 1973. The original cottage is on the left, the right hand extension having been added just after the '39 – '45 war. Peak's Brickhouse was situated behind the cottage and since its demolition the site has been converted for use as a riding school.

Wilderswood Mill – Circa 1895. Wilderswood House and stables can be seen to the left of the mill. Factory Hill Cottages which housed mill-workers can be seen to the right. The whitewashed building in the lower right of this picture is Mill Hole cottage.

Wilderswood House is presently used as a dwelling and although the mill was demolished in 1911 and the cottages in 1939, traces of them can still be seen.

Wilderswood Mill – Circa 1887. This early photograph gives some idea of the size of the Mill.

CHAPTER 10

The Scotsman's Murder

It is almost 150 years ago since George Henderson, aged 20 years, a native of Annan, Dumfrieshire, was shot dead on Horwich Moor at a point near to where the Winter Hill IBA Transmitter Station now stands. The brief circumstances of the murder are that Henderson was employed as a travelling packman by William Jardine, a Blackburn draper. The work involved travelling certain rounds to sell his employer's goods, taking orders for the same and collecting money.

Benjamin Birrell, also a scotsman, was employed in a similar capacity by another Blackburn Draper, John Foster. Both Henderson and Birrell crossed Horwich Moor about the same time every other Friday and, not unnaturally, they became friends and would arrange to meet and travel back to Blackburn together, where they would account the fortnights business transactions with their respective employers.

On Friday 9th November 1838, the two men had made just such an arrangement to meet at the 'Five Houses' beer-house on Horwich Moor at 11 o'clock in the morning. Birrell reached the 'Five Houses' first, about 10 a.m., and stayed till just after 11 a.m. at which time Henderson had still not arrived, so he decided to go on alone, leaving word with Mrs Garbutt, the landlord's wife, to inform Henderson when he eventually

turned up. As Birrel continued on his way over the moor he saw a man carrying a gun who came up to him and asked if he had seen two men. Some conversation then followed before Birrell resumed his journey. On glancing back over his shoulder Birrell saw the same man about ten yards behind with the gun aimed towards him. The man asked Birrell if he had just seen some birds rise nearby, which he had not. There was then a further exchange of words before Birrell once again set off for Belmont.

George Henderson got to 'Five Houses' about 12 noon and Mrs Garbutt passed on Birrell's message. He only stayed a short time, leaving about quarter past twelve. As Henderson left the beer-house Thomas Whowell, a 14 year old boy, was passing on horseback. The time was confirmed because the boy had heard Ridgway's factory bell (Wallsuches Bleachworks) ringing midday. Whowell was taking dinner to his brother who worked at a nearby coal pit. His horse was walking very slowly and Henderson easily managed to keep pace, maintaining an even distance behind all the way to the mine. On arrival, the boy dismounted and swore at the horse because it would not stand still. By this time Henderson had arrived at the spot and mildly chastised the boy for this, then carried on walking. After staying at the mine for about ten minutes Whowell went upon his way walking behind the horse. He had gone about 300 yards when he saw blood on the roadway and heard moans coming from a drainage ditch by the side of the road. Realising that something dreadful had happened, and being too frightened to look further, the boy went for help.

James Fletcher was working nearby on a coal outcrop known as 'The Tunnel' and Whowell told him what he had seen. Fletcher hastened to the spot indicated by the boy where he saw George Henderson lying face upwards in the drainage ditch with the water flowing over his belly. There were terrible injuries to Henderson's face, one eye had been completely blown out of its socket and the other lay on his cheek. Fletcher was unable to lift Henderson from the ditch unaided and further assistance was therefore summoned. Several persons eventually carried Henderson to the 'Five Houses' while a doctor was called, but he died about 2 p.m. that day.

William Jardine offered a reward of £100 for information leading to the arrest and conviction of the person(s) responsible for the murder of his employee.

MURDER
AND ROBBERY.
100 POUNDS REWARD

WHEREAS,

A Cruel and Atrocious Murder and Robbery was committed on the person of GEORGE HENDERSON, a Traveller, between Five Houses and Belmont, on FRIDAY last, the 9th Instant, who was Shot at with a GUN.

This is to give Notice,

That a REWARD of One Hundred Pounds, will be given to any Person or Persons, who, after this date, shall give such information as may lead to the detection and conviction of the Murderer or Murderers, by applying to

MR. WILLIAM JARDINE,
JOHN STREET, BLACKBURN.

Blackburn, November 11th, 1838.

J. BURRELL, PRINTER, GAZETTE-OFFICE, CHURCH STREET, BLACKBURN.

On Tuesday 13th November 1838, four days after the murder, an inquest was held at the Horwich Moor-Gate Inn, which is the former title of the Blundell Arms. The Coroner, William Smalley Rutter, sat with a jury of seventeen local men and evidence was heard from twenty two witnesses. During the two day inquest it emerged that Henderson had allegedly said "I am robbed, I am killed" indicating that robbery was the motive for the murder. Several witnesses had seen James Whittle, a 22 year old collier who lived in the same terraced row as the 'Five Houses', carrying a gun close to where Henderson was shot.

The Blundell Arms (formerly the Horwich Moor-Gate Inn) Chorley Old Road, Horwich. (Photograph Circa 1900). The Blundell Arms derives its name from the Blundell family who were substantial landowners in the Horwich area until early this century. Local families who made their livelihood in the bleaching industry rented crofts from the Blundell's and rental dues were paid at the pub. The inquest on the murder of George Henderson was held here in November 1838.

Matthew Lambert, the landlord at the Horwich Moor-Gate Inn, told the inquest that he had loaned a single barrelled percussion cap rifle to Whittle on Thursday 8th November, the day before the murder. They had arranged to go shooting in Brownlow's Close, which is behind the Moor-Gate, on Friday afternoon.

About 1.30 p.m. on Friday 9th November, Whittle arrived at the Moor-Gate with a brace of freshly shot grouse. He returned the rifle along with a gunpowder flask and a bag of shot which had been loaned to him two years previously. Whittle said that a neighbour named

Orrell was always complaining about him shooting and he was determined to give it up.

Birrell was unable to make a positive identification of Whittle as the man who pointed the gun at him but nevertheless the inquest jury returned a verdict of 'wilful murder' against Whittle at which he is reported to have burst into tears.

George Henderson was buried at the Presbyterian Chapel at Mount Street, Blackburn, on the second day of the inquest and a large crowd of mourners turned out to pay their last respects.

Whittle stood trial for murder on the 2nd April 1839, at the Lancashire Lent Assizes held in Liverpool. The case gainst him hinged principally on the evidence of Joseph Halliwell. He was a Yorkshireman by birth who worked for a Bolton cattle dealer named Gerrard. On the day of the murder he had set off on horseback from Bolton to buy a heifer from a person called Walsh. Due to poor directions he visited Gilligants Farm where he spoke to a Mrs Hood who put him on the road for Belmont. The day was foggy and Halliwell lost his way on the moor. Hearing the report of a gun Halliwell made his way towards the sound with the intention of asking whoever was shooting, the way. About fifteen minutes later he saw a man running 'very hard' towards him. The man passed within five yards and he was carrying a gun in his right hand. Halliwell accurately described the dress of this man and when asked by the prosecuting counsel if he was sure that Whittle was the same man he replied. "I am sure he is, so help me God". Some three hundred yards further along the road Halliwell came across Henderson who was lying mortally wounded in a ditch. He dismounted and on seeing the terrible injuries to Henderson, and being afraid that he would be implicated, left him to his fate.

During cross-examination Halliwell lost all credibility due to his trucculent and prevaricatory manner. He contradicted himself several times and made the sinister claim that he was given a piece of the dead man's skull near to the scene of the murder by an Irishman and woman. Following the discovery of Henderson's body, Halliwell called at the 'Five Houses' where he consumed a drink while seated on his horse. After leaving there he went to the Duckworth Arms at Over Darwen between Bolton and Blackburn. He remembered showing the piece of skull to the licensee, James Proctor.

The prosecution case finished at 5.45 p.m. and the judge refused a defence request to adjourn the hearing to the following morning although he granted a one hour recess. Defence submissions and the judges summing up concluded at 9 p.m. and the jury retired to consider their verdict. After an hour and a quarter a verdict of 'Not Guilty' was returned and the foreman of the jury commented that it was in consequence of the defective evidence of Halliwell. Whittle was therefore discharged a free man and His Lordship remarked that the jury had taken the safest side.

Whittle was reputedly an expert marksman who put up his skills for money at game shooting competitions. There is a story that following his acquittal for the alleged murder of Henderson he failed to come up to the standard usually expected of him in a shoot at Belmont, resulting in his backers losing their stake money. One of these disappointed men commented that Whittle's shooting had been better when he shot the scotsman. This remark resulted in Whittle withdrawing from the sport never to shoot again and he became a recluse. He eventually lost his sight and died in middle age a broken man. It is believed that following Whittle's death on the 6th April 1871 he was buried in Horwich Parish Church graveyard.

The Scotsman's Post

The Scotsman's Post is a memorial to George Henderson and stands opposite the Winter Hill Transmitter Station marking the spot on the moor where George Henderson met his death. Shortly after the murder a tree was planted but this was removed in 1912 to make way for a cast iron pillar bearing an inscribed plate. The cost of erection was met by public subscription. In recent years the original plate became so weather worn that a replacement was cast and affixed to the post. There is a contention that the post also acts as a reminder that there has been a public right of way over the moor since 1838.

Scotsman's Stump showing original plate.

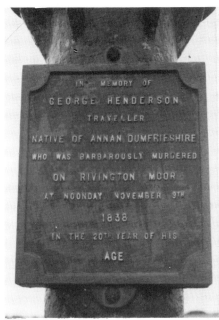

Replacement plate.

The portrait of James Whittle which appeared in the 1838 newspaper found recently in a Bamber Bridge cottage attic.

"It was while groping about in the roofspace at his cottage home in Chorley Road, Bamber Bridge, that Mr Gordon Hunt came across an old newspaper.

On spreading out the parched, yellow sheets, he found it was a copy of the former Blackburn Gazette dated November 1838. The leading story of the paper was headed Horrible Murder on Horwich Moor.

Gordon and his wife Margaret moved into the old oak-beamed cottage about a year ago and it was formerly part of the de Hoghton estate."

CHAPTER 11
ROCKHAVEN CASTLE

Arguably, one of the most memorable features of the Horwich landscape was Rockhaven Castle. The property was developed from 1840 by Richard Brownlow, an attorney of Wood Street, Bolton, who was the son of Christopher Brownlow of Manor House, Horwich. Richard Brownlow was a keen horseman who together with Mr Munday of Preston founded the Horwich Races. Horse racing was originally staged in a field below Wilderswood Farm until a purpose built track was eventually constructed on the banks of the River Douglas at Old Lords.

In later life Richard Brownlow became something of a recluse mainly due to a facial disfigurement caused by erysipelas, he did, however, continue to hold parties at the Castle but on these occasions he wore a face mask. Following his death in 1899 Rockhaven Castle was purchased by Lord Leverhulme.

The property was demolished in 1942.

Rockhaven Castle – Circa 1912.

Some say that the reason was because it provided an ideal fixing point for German bombers trying to disable the war effort at Horwich Locomotive Works. A proportion of the stonework from the Castle was used to build a bungalow in Lytham while the remainder was carried as ballast in grain ships travelling to America. All the area around the castle grounds has been afforested and it is now difficult to imagine that this architecturally striking building once stood there.

Rockhaven Castle (viewed from the north-west) – 1908. View of Rockhaven Castle taken from a post card which was postally used in 1908. An antique dealer named Hignett who had business premises in Prince's Arcade once occupied the Castle. During his tenancy the glass conservatory (shown left) was opened to the public as a tea room.

Rockhaven Castle from George's Lane with Rivington Pike in the background.

CHAPTER 12
The Railway Comes to Town

The railway line from Bolton to Black-rod and Chorley was opened in 1841 with four service trains running each day Monday to Saturday and two on Sundays. The trains left Bolton at 8.15 a.m., 11.00 a.m. and 2.15 p.m. and 6.00 p.m. during the week and on Sunday at 8.30 a.m. and 6.30 p.m. respectively. The fare for the journey was – first class 1s

6d, second class 10d and third class 8d, with special rates on Sunday when second class travel was charged at the third class rate.

On the 22nd May 1866 the L & YR awarded a £30,400 contract to Garside and Stead for the construction of a railway line connecting Hindley, Blackrod and Horwich including a railway station

Blackrod Railway Station – Circa 1897.

at Horwich. The link was opened for goods traffic on the 15th July 1868 but passenger traffic did not commence using it until the 14th February 1870.

Blackrod Railway Station is situated

about one mile from Horwich town centre and the opening of Horwich Station to passenger traffic in 1870 saved the long walk from Horwich Vale up Station Road and Crown Lane to Crown Square.

Vale House, off Crown Lane, Horwich – 1905

Crown Lane looking towards Crown Square – 1919.

Crown Lane looking towards Blackrod – 1910

Station Road, Horwich Junction – Circa 1905.

Crown Lane, Horwich – 1916.

Horwich Railway Station Staff – 1910.

CHAPTER 13
A Nation of Shopkeepers

"We are indeed a nation of shopkeepers" is a saying attributed to Benjamin Disraeli – Earl of Beaconsfield (1804 – 1881) who was Prime Minister in 1868 and again from 1874 to 1880. An eight foot high stone statue of Disraeli once stood on the roof apex in front of the Conservative Club in Church Street. It has now gone and is believed to be buried in a quarry off Crown Lane.

Church Street, Horwich – Circa 1897. The Conservative Club can be seen on the right and the statue of Disraeli is directly above the people on the balcony.

Butchers

'The butcher, the baker and the candlestick maker' is a term which exemplifies the diversity of small shop-keeping concerns. There was no problem in providing illustrations for the two former but candlestickmakers are a difficult proposition. However, in 1885 Mr Bentley of Upper Horwich made six candlesticks for Father Hampson and carried them to Gorton Fold in a sack so that the first Mass in Horwich could be celebrated.

Wilkinson's Butcher's Shop, Lee Lane, Horwich – Circa 1890.
Mrs Wilkinson is standing to the right.

Kay's Butcher's Shop, Lee Lane, Horwich – 1952. The shop was run by three generations of the same family. James Kay started the business in 1886, his son Anyon took over in 1917 and grandson Gordon (see above) in 1952.

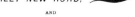

46, *Winter Hey Lane,*
Horwich, Sep 22nd 1921

Mr W. Holding Bro

Bought of A. W. MARKLAND,
FAMILY BUTCHER.

Accounts Monthly.   :   5% charged on overdue accounts.

Jan 15/1921 Red Cow	60 - 0 - 0
" "	52 - 0 - 0
Bay Horse	35 - 0 - 0
Blue Dog	1 - 10 - 0
Jan 28 Roaned Cow	52 - 0 - 0
Red & White cow	25 - 0 - 0
Feb 5 three popped cow	38 - 10 - 0
	264 - 0 - 0
Feb 5 Red Cow	22 - 0 - 0
	242 - 0 - 0
April 16 Red /Polly	48 - 0 - 0
May 21 Exchange Pig	5 - 0 - 0
June 10 Red Cow	52 - 0 - 0
July 30 Roaned Cow	38 - 0 - 0
	385 - 0 - 0

Anyon A Kay's Butchery Van – Circa 1920.

Bakers

Waddicor's Cake Shop, 33 Lee Lane, Horwich – Circa 1906. The Waddicor family kept a confectionery shop at 33 Lee Lane from 1897 to 1911. This close up view of the display windows was intended to make the mouth water although the two wedding cakes were probably cardboard replicas intended to advertise their icing skills.

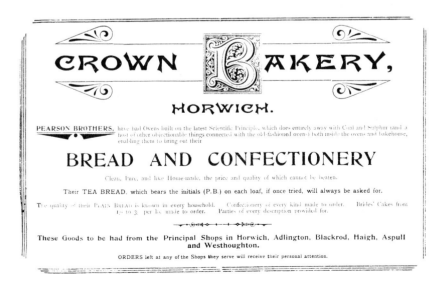

Other Businesses

X-L Shoe Shop, 36 Lee Lane, Horwich – 1904.

Pendlebury's Baby Linen Shop, 27 Winter Hey Lane, Horwich – Circa 1908. Mrs Pendlebury is standing at the door of her shop. It is now occupied by Greeley's butchery.

Valentine's Newsagents and Tobacconists Shop, 64 Lee Lane, Horwich – Circa 1935. This shop stands where the lodge for Purl Brook Works was once situated. It serviced the immediate area around Brownlow Road.

Lee Lane, Horwich – 1910.

Bromley's Sweet Shop, Lee Lane, Horwich – Circa 1935. Gladys Bromley is pictured outside her sweet shop which was on the corner of Lord Street opposite the Bowling Green Inn.

Chorley New Road, Horwich – Circa 1950.

Crown Square, Horwich – Circa 1925.

Winter Hey Lane, Horwich – Circa 1940.

Horwich Co-operative Society

The first Co-operative shop in Horwich was the front room of Mary Chalonder's stone cottage at 126 Lee Lane, which opened for business in 1862. In spite of such humble beginnings trade quickly became established and larger premises were soon needed. A rental was then taken out on 140 Lee Lane.

The cottage the Society first used.

The second shop.

These new premises also proved in-adequate and so in 1865 a brand new central store was constructed on Lee Lane. A man and a boy were employed full time at the central store. On Sundays they were responsible for feeding the pigs kept behind the shop.

The first central premises on Lee Lane – Circa 1910.

Brownlow Road, Horwich – 1919

Horses from the Co-op Stables in Harrison Street, Horwich – 1912.

Horwich Taxi – Circa 1920.

Tea House, Heaviley Grove, Horwich – Circa 1910.

In common with many other business concerns the arrival of the Horwich Locomotive Works brought unprecedented expansion. The Society speculated on the property market constructing fourteen houses in Brownlow Road and developing Pioneer Street on land behind.

Branches of the Co-op sprang up all over Horwich. In 1891 land was purchased adjoining Chorley New Road from the Lancashire and Yorkshire Railway for the erection of five branch shops and a bakehouse. A shop was also opened on Church Street that year and one in Lee Lane the following year. Stabling was provided for the Co-op horses in Harrison Street where a slaughterhouse and porkery were also run. Further branches included one in Crown Lane opened in 1898, Bottom o'th Moor purchased in 1907 and two houses in George Street purchased in 1900 and converted into a butchery and a clogger's shop, respectively.

At a monthly meeting held on the 2nd April 1900 it was resolved "That the Committee be empowered to purchase land or buildings for the Central premises in Lee Lane for Butchery, Boots and Furniture Departments". A number of old buildings were purchased in Lee Lane for £565 and these were demolished to make way for the new Central Store. The two storey building comprised a Secretary's Office, Newsroom, Boardroom and Showroom and the Furnishing Department – upstairs, a Butcher's; Boots and Furnishing shop – downstairs; with a workshop for the shoemakers and cloggers at the rear. Although no longer operating as a Co-operative Store the premises are still easily identifiable by an elephant and the date 1902 cast in terra-cotta on the raised parapet at the front.

New Central Premises – 1912

CHAPTER 14

Horwich at the time of the Crimean War

Crown Square, Horwich – Post Card view postally used in January 1904.

In March 1854 Britain and France declared war on Russia in defence of Turkey. The Russian Tsar had announced plans to partition Turkish territory and in pursuit of this objective had destroyed the Turkish fleet at Sinope on the 30th November 1853. With true 'gun-boat' diplomacy British and French warships were ordered into the Black Sea to prevent the Russians

landing on Turkish soil. The Allies themselves landed on the Crimean Peninsula in September 1854 and for 12 months laid siege to the town of Sebastopol. While the siege was in progress, in fact during the first two months of it, the famous battles of Inkerman and Balaclava took place. Appalling administration and logistical arrangements resulted in much unnecessary loss of life

94

which was relieved only by the nursing activities of Florence Nightingale. Peace was provisionally agreed on the 1st February 1856 when the Austrians threatened to join the Allies and was ratified at the Congress of Paris a few weeks later.

The Crimean War awoke national fervour and people were anxious for details from the front although communication in the 1850's was a slow process with news taking weeks to spread. The population of Horwich at this time was 3,000 and there was neither a newsagents or a stationers shop to service the populace. A woman known as 'Old Lady Higginson' came from Bolton twice a week, on Wednesday and Saturday, with newspapers and periodicals which were eagerly snapped up.

Horwich Post Office was then situated near to the Crown Hotel and all

The Black Bull Hotel, Church Street, Horwich – Circa 1905. The original lease was granted on the 29th September 1775 and the premises were built on Glebe (Church) land belonging to Horwich Parish Church. Thomas Hampson in the 'History of Horwich' makes the following reference to the Black Bull Hotel:–

"The parlour of the Black Bull was the sanctum sanctorum (Holy of Holies) of village politicians. Within it Mr Ridgway held his court; within it churchwarden and constable broke the law while looking for law breakers. The landlord of the Black Bull was an important personage. He was the repository of many secrets, and knew the outcome of village councils. Its connection with the church gave it a status that overshadowed its licensed authority, and made it the rendezvous of all sections of the community. The local aristocrats drank at its bar, and the village crofter gathered in its tap room".

deliveries and collections of mail were transacted there. A foot messenger walked from Bolton each morning, returning during the evening. Letters and parcels were only delivered to premises along the route in exceptional circumstances by special request.

Mr Scott was the landlord of the Black

Bull Hotel at this time and seized on the idea of having the Manchester and London newspapers specially delivered to the pub. Locals flocked to the Black Bull to hear the latest war news and this ritual continued for the duration of hostilities.

Whenever good news arrived from the battle-front appropriate celebrations were staged. Flags were made from calico supplied by Wallsuches and the Vale Print Works, although the French tri-colour and the Turkish star and crescent flag were more in evidence than the Union flag, simply because the two former flags were much easier to make. As the conflict progressed there were several occasions to celebrate the Allied successes, notably the fall of Sebastopol on the 11th September, 1855.

Following the cessation of hostilities, victory celebrations were organised throughout Horwich. A home made cannon, constructed from the ram of a hydraulic press mounted on a four wheeled locomotive waggon bogey, was to be used for a Royal 21 gun salute. The gun barrel was 4 feet long and 12 inches in diameter with a quarter inch touch hole drilled in the breach. Two old Waterloo veterans, John Gee and W Whittle, had responsibility for charging and firing the cannon which was placed near to Wallsuches Bleachworks. The gun had a tremendous recoil on being fired and it proved such a slow process to replace it after each shot that during the intervals between firing the crowd was entertained by the Ridgway Band.

Aerial view of Wallsuches Bleachworks – 1925.

Joseph Rawlinson was a boy at the time and later recorded some of his experiences, including a description of the celebrations which took place in Horwich after the Allied victory in the Crimean War. Coincidentally, a man named Rawlinson who lived in Prospect House, New Chapel, was engineman at Wallsuches Bleachworks about 1900 but it is not certain that he is the same person.

On that particular day, while the festivities were in full swing, James Radcliffe, the licensee of the Sportsman's Arms near to Rivington Pike, promised to give rushes to Rawlinson and some of his friends provided they called to collect them at the pub, (in those days rushes were used as floor covering). Towards evening, when the cannon at Wallsuches had completed its fusilade, Joseph set off for the Sports-

Mr Rawlinson of Prospect House, New Chapel who was engineman at Wallsuches Bleachworks about 1900.

man's Arms with a number of other boys.

Nearing the summit of the Pike the boys were spoken to by James Worsley an old 'keeper' who, out of concern for the youths, asked them where they were going. Joseph told Mr Worsley that

they were on the way to the Pike Tower to listen to the bells and after some persuasion Worsley agreed to accompany the lads to the top. The sun was then setting and this coupled with the sound of innumerable church bells gave the place an air of enchantment. "Listen

Rivington Pike Tower – Circa 1910.

Mr Worsley, listen to the bells" said the boys, "they seem to be ringing inside the Tower." The gruff old man thought a while and with some emotion in his voice said, "Aye, they're bonny lads, they're bonny, but there's many a poor lad in the Crimea will never hear those bells no more."

As the bitter sweet moment passed Mr Worsley advised the boys to make their way home and they did so, calling at the Sportsman's Arms on the way to collect their rushes. On arriving at the Inn, Mr Radcliffe supplied the promised rushes and the boys thanked him and then prevailed upon him to play the hurdy-gurdy. He refused saying that it was late but promised to do so another time. The Sportsman's Arms and the Bridge Hotel were the only two licensed premises out of twelve in Horwich which provided entertainment, in the form of a hurdy-gurdy and a violin respectively. (A hurdy-gurdy is a musical instrument with a distincitive droning sound which is played by turning a handle).

The Bridge Hotel, Church Street, Horwich – 1903. The Bridge Hotel was the second pub of the same name to be constructed on this site. Its predecessor was relatively small and before the enlarged premises could be built the licences of two smaller public houses had to be surrendered. This requirement was necessary to prevent the proliferation of licensed houses in the district. In the event, the two Justices' licences relinquished belonged to the former Bridge Hotel and the Sportsman's Arms on Rivington Moor, respectively. For a long number of years the Calderbank family held the licence for the Bridge Hotel and they also ran the Bridgefoot Smithy but this was eventually sold to the Milner family.

Milner's Bridgefoot Smithy – Circa 1890. The Smithy was continually operated for 200 years but as motor transport replaced horses, light engineering and wrought ironwork replaced farriery. An embrocation known as 'Milner's Athletes' Rub' was once sold from the Smithy which on application is alleged to have smelled worse than a red hot shoe being applied to a horses's hoof. The building was demolished a few years ago during road widening.

The Milner family at work – 1910. Mr Milner is standing, arms akimbo, to the left and his two sons are shoeing the horse.

The Bridge Hotel – Circa 1880.

CHAPTER 15
The Flagpole on Horwich Parish Church

Horwich Parish Church – 1935.

On the same evening that the clientele of the Black Bull were discussing the Allied victory in the Crimean War, it was commented that there was not a colour or a flag pole in Horwich, and one should be provided at the Parish Church. William Longworth, known locally as Squire Longworth, was in the company and as peoples' warden at the church he was asked if the vicar, Reverend Pigot, would object. The matter had been discussed previously among the wardens, and the vicar was strongly in favour of such a scheme.

On receiving Longworth's reassurance a collection was organised and an appropriate sum of money was quickly provided. Mr Scott, the landlord of the Black Bull, agreed to act as treasurer of the fund and Squire Longworth under-

101

took the arrangements for the purchase of a suitable flagstaff.

A ship's mast was eventually obtained from Liverpool and delivered to Horwich Parish Church. By far the most difficult task was yet to be overcome, the hoisting of the flagpole to the top of the church tower. Several mechanics said that it was impossible but Nicholas Holden, a manager for R Harrison at Pilkington Quarry, was confident that it could be done. Under Holden's supervision, seven or eight quarrymen using ropes and blocks slowly hauled the flagstaff up the tower. The copper crown measuring 2 feet 6 inches wide by 1 foot 9 inches deep was affixed as the top of the pole reached the tower roof. When it was finally positioned stays of iron manufactured at Calderbanks Smithy were put in place, resulting in the erection of a most satisfactory standard pole. Although the copper crown was eventually removed due to storm damage, surprisingly, it was never struck by lightning.

Reverend H S Pigot, Vicar of Horwich Parish Church.

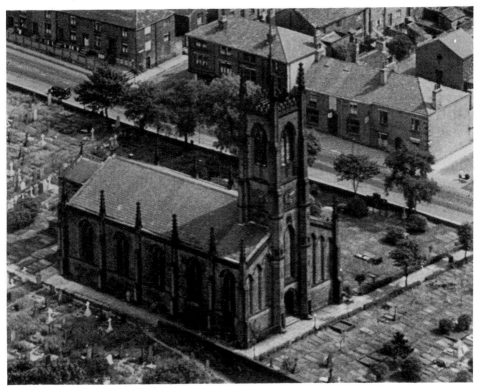

Aerial view of Horwich Parish Church.

CHAPTER 16
The Church is one foundation

"To write even a summary of the history of Methodism in Horwich is to write a history of the village" – so wrote Thomas Hampson in 1883. Sadly this is not the case a hundred years on. Several of the chapels which were standing then have either been demolished or put to some other purpose. However, others have been built to take their place and many faiths are now represented which is a healthy sign of religious tolerance.

Reference to a number of churches and church schools is included.

St Catherine's Church & School, Horwich

The foundation stone for St Catherine's Church was laid by the Earl of Lathom on the 2nd October 1897. The picture of this event speaks volumes in respect of the interest it generated among the townsfolk.

Laying the foundation stone for St Catherine's Church, Horwich.

St Catherine's Church.

St Catherine's School, Horwich – 1880 – A mixed class of pupils with Mr Field, Headmaster on left.

New Chapel & Sunday School, New Chapel Lane, Horwich

There was a building of some sort used for worship at New Chapel as early as 1690 although the original Trust Deed only dates back to 1719. 'New Chapel' was a meeting house for dissenters and was so named to distinguish it from the 'Old Chapel', as the Parish Church of Horwich was formerly known. Its isolated position is attributed to the Five Mile Act 1665. This legislation prevented any clergyman or schoolmaster who would not conform to an edict of Charles II and swear that it was not lawful, upon any pretence whatever to take arms against the King, or try to secure any alteration of government either in Church or State; from coming within five miles of any City, Corporation or place where they had preached.

The history of New Chapel therefore spans well over 250 years. Numbered among its congregation have been many notable Horwich families including the Whittles, the Pilkingtons and the Greenhalghs. Since the Chapel was built it has been extensively altered and enlarged. A Sunday School was added in the late eighteenth century. This has also since been renovated.

New Chapel lane – 1901. This was a private roadway leading to New Chapel. The gate across the roadway gave the area the name 'Whitegate'. Visible back left is New Chapel House, once occupied by a branch of the Pilkington family.

New Chapel, Horwich – 1920. The roof cupola shown here has now been removed from the building.

New Chapel Sunday School – 1935.

New Independent Methodist's Church, Lee Lane, Horwich

The foundation stone laying ceremony for the New Independent Methodist's Church took place on the 25th August 1906. Increase in the population following the opening of Horwich Locomotive Works had prompted the need for an

New Independent Methodists' Church – 1910.

Group 9 Independent Methodists' Day School – Circa 1910.

expanded church and the 'new' building augmented an existing Methodist Church built in 1867. Two church schools were also built in 1884 and 1888 respectively.

Victoria Methodist Chapel, Church Street, Horwich

Woodhouse and Morley, Architects of Bolton, were appointed to build Victoria Methodist Chapel in Gothic design and of Yorkshire stone. The foundation stone was laid on 6th April 1887 and the building was named 'Victoria' Chapel to commemorate fifty years of Queen Victoria's reign. There were delays in construction

and the eventual cost was £7,000 as against the original estimate of £4,000. On the 8th March 1888, the Chapel was opened and the inaugural service was conducted by the Reverend Charles Garrett.

Trustees of the Lancashire and Yorkshire Railway Company were approached to see if they would assist in the upkeep of a Day School if one was built. For a variety of reasons they were reluctant to do so but a school was finally opened on the 8th November 1890.

Both the chapel and the school were demolished for residential property development in the early 1970's.

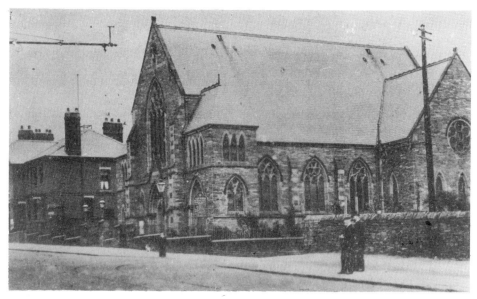

Victoria Methodist Chapel – 1903.

Victoria Methodist Sunday School – 1901. A group of Sunday School children photographed outside Victoria Methodists' Church.

Lee Lane Congregational Chapel – Circa 1890.

Livesey's Waggonette outside Lee lane Congregational Church – 1929. Livesey's Waggonette is seen here on Lee Lane outside the Congregational Church. A comparison with the earlier view reveals that the front building has been removed and the rear one substantially altered. The fine pair of Belgian horses were bought from Miss Lucy Howarth of Wallsuches House just prior to her leaving the district to live in Bournemouth.

Lee Lane Congregational Chapel, Horwich

Oliver John Milton, author of Paradise Lost, was Cromwell's secretary and argued against the conception of the Blessed Trinity. This teaching was known as 'Socinianism' and in the mid seventeenth century the doctrine was being preached at Rivington Chapel. Several objectors broke away and for a while met for prayer and worship in a dingle or stone quarry at the base of Rivington Pike. About 1770 four of the breakaway group, Hugh Makinson, Moses Cocker, Thomas Anderton and John Ashworth, established a small separate church in Rivington which was used until 1774 when the foundation stone for Lee Lane Congregational Chapel was laid. In 1856 this chapel was replaced by a larger one designed by George Woodhouse and built by Mr Pickersgill at a cost of £1,500. Seating accommodation was provided for 600 persons.

Spiritualist Church and Lyceum, Chorley New Road, Horwich

The church stands directly opposite St Mary's Church.

St Mary's, Chorley New Road, Horwich

Prior to the arrival of Horwich Locomotive Works there were less than 200 practising Catholics in the town who having no church of their own were obliged to travel to neighbouring towns and villages to worship. The majority

Horwich Spiritualist Church and Lyceum – inside view – Circa 1920. The church stands directly opposite St Mary's Church.

Lee Lane Horwich – Circa 1903. Mason Memorial Chapel is on the right hand side.

Chorley New Road Council School – Circa 1900.

used to attend services at St Joseph's Church. Anderton, which has existed since 1863.

In anticipation of a dramatic population increase following the arrival of the Locomotive Works, with a proportionate rise in the number of Catholics; Bishop Vaughan of Salford decided to establish Horwich as a parish in its own right and commenced enquiries to obtain a suitable site on which to build a church and school for use by its parishioners.

On the 25th March, a large tract of land on the south side of Chorley New Road was leased for a period of 999 years. The lessor was Mrs Julia Catherine Wright, wife of Frederick D'Arley Wright of Mottram Hall, Cheshire. Such was the gratitude of local Catholics that Julia, Catherine, Wright, Frederick, Darley and Mottram Streets were named in honour of them. A Catholic church was opened on the 11th July 1886 and the integral 'Our Lady's' school on the 19th July 1886. The present St Mary's Church was built in 1905.

Procession of Witness, St Mary's Church. Horwich – early 1960's.

Horwich Spiritualist Church is the single storey building to the left of the tram.

The original Roman Catholic Church and 'Our Lady of the Rosary' School can be seen on the left of this photograph – Circa 1902.

CHAPTER 17

Horwich Public Hall

At a meeting held in the 'Old School', Church Street, on Wednesday 14th February 1877, to discuss the gift of £112.17s.8d. from the Lee Mill ground rent for the benefit of the people of Horwich, Mr A Mason suggested that the money should go towards providing a social centre containing a public subscription library and reading rooms together with facilities for staging con-

certs and other forms of amusement. In March 1877 at a reconvened meeting Mr Peter Martin of 'The Street' Rivington, a successful cotton magnate who owned several mills in the district, announced that he was prepared to erect a building at his own expense on Lee Lane; provided that it should be opened free from debt, the general public being asked to subscribe; and that it should not be used

The photograph taken about 1902 shows the Public Hall with a flagpole at the front. Lee Lane is cobbled and the tram tracks confirm the date between 1900 – 1907.

for denominational purposes but be governed by a representative committee to be revised every five or seven years. The proposal was accepted and in 1878 the Public Hall on Lee Lane was built. It is described in Hampson's History of Horwich as follows:–

"The Hall covers an area of 32 superficial yards, and the offices, stables and outbuildings cover a further space 136 yards. The bowling green is 52 yards by 36. The view from the outside is delightful, the hills forming a kind of background to the lovely landscape. The general style of the building is of the Gothic design, Elizabethan type. The front is extremely attractive, being of pressed brick relieved by terra cotta tracery; the apex being of Yorkshire stone. The interior of the building is in keeping with its outward aspect, the

The Common Seal of Horwich Local Board. The device has two men bearing staffs, with a stag in the centre, above being the Royal Crown, the motto being "Labour is Wealth".

handsome staircase of polished pitch-pine, together with the other appointments being most harmonious. On the ground floor is the billiard room, reading rooms, chess and draughts room and coffee room, over which is a large assembly room of 1,505 square feet, the most striking feature of the building, perhaps, being the turret, surmounted by a weather vane, from which project the points of the compass".

The Public Hall was officially opened on the 2nd April 1879 but, unfortunately, Peter Martin only survived the ceremony a few months. In 1882 his wife, Mary, presented the building for the town's use.

Local government arrived in Horwich when the town adopted the Local Government Act 1858. The Horwich Local Board was formed on the 15th

August 1872 and the common seal of the Board bore the motto 'Labour is Wealth'.

The first meeting of the Board took place at the National School on the 16th October 1872 and these premises conti-nued in use for this purpose until the Public Hall became available following its demise as a social centre. For a number of years the Public Hall was the focal point for all social events in Horwich but when the Lancashire and Yorkshire Railway Company opened the Mechanic's

Lee Lane, Horwich – 1905.

Institute on the 15th December 1888, its popularity began to decline.

Following the implementation of the Local Government Act 1894, the Horwich Local Board was re-constituted as the Horwich Urban District Council. John Longworth was its first elected chairman and the inaugural meeting took place in the Public Hall Council Chambers on the 9th January 1895. Since this time the Council Chambers have been successively used by the Horwich Town Council, formed on the 1st April 1974 with the Greater Manchester Metropolitan County, and by the present Council since the GMC was disbanded on the 1st April 1986.

Coat of Arms – Present day.

The present Coat of Arms features a deer and huntsman, two red Lancashire roses separated by a pair of black railway lines with the Pilkington family cross between them. The original motto has been retained although the translation is now 'Industry brings Prosperity'.

(By kind permission of Horwich Town Council).

The distinctive weather vane atop the Public Hall can be seen on the left – 1909.

CHAPTER 18

'Industry brings Prosperity'

Horwich's motto 'Industry brings Prosperity' is a realisation that success is only achieved by dint of human effort. There is no illusion that anyone will be fortunate enough to be born with the proverbial 'silver spoon' in their mouth.

The streams flowing from the water catchment area on the moors above

Thomas Hampson – author of 'History of Horwich'.

Horwich and the underlying sandstone, coal and clay have all been harnessed to support a wide variety of industries; including mining, quarrying, textile manufacture, brick and earthenware works, and papermaking.

Generations of Horwich folk have had to work virtually all their lives, in some cases from being below school age to their late seventies and eighties. Local historian Thomas Hampson, well known for his 'History of Horwich', was born in 1839 and started work at Wallsuches Bleachworks when he was only seven years old. He lost a number of fingers on his left hand in a works accident which seems to have forced him into a clerical career. The short lived Red Moss

View across Horwich – Circa 1900. This photograph gives some idea of the number of factories which once operated in Horwich. Higher Meadows Farm can be seen front centre with Rockhaven Castle far left. Horwich Parish Church tower is visible back left. The two chimneys in front of Blackrod Reservoir belonged to Andrew Peak's Brickworks and the group of three chimneys back right indicate W Pickup's enamelled fireclay works. Tall chimneys can be a hazard as the photograph of Crown Brickworks shows.

Ironworks saw his services as a secretary. This was followed by periods of employment as a cashier, first at Scot Lane Colliery then at Fourgates Colliery. He last worked as a clerk on the Locomotive Works. His death occurred at Bolton Royal Infirmary on the 25th November 1918.

Environmental pollution is now a serious concern and it is difficult to appreciate how industrialised the Horwich District once was. Even on a sunny summer's day the town would be shrouded in a grey haze. Fortunately the clear moorland air above the town always provided an escape.

Crown Brickworks chimney was devastated by lightning during a thunderstorm on the 25th May 1909. A number of bricks were blown onto the roof of St Mary's Church causing damage.

John Crankshaw, Pipe Works

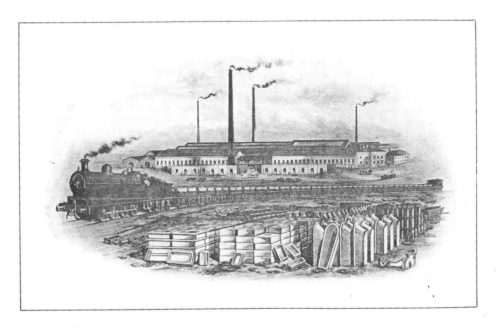

Pearl Brook Works, Horwich – 1917

Makinson's Timber Yard, St John Street, Horwich. The workers at Makinson's Timber Yard, St John Street off Winter Hey Lane, Horwich doing their bit to help the 1914-18 war effort.

Advertising postcard for Wm Makinson & Sons.

Telford Mill – Circa 1915 – Romeo Foster Proprietor.

Messrs W T Taylor & Co, Victoria Mills, Chorley New Road, Horwich. The towel mill offices can be seen extreme left.

Montcliffe Mine showing the wooden headstock.

Montcliffe Mine with the replacement headstock and metal winding gear.

Montcliffe Quarry – The coal mine headstock can be seen left of centre.

Montcliffe Coal Mine

It is said that the coal in the hillsides above Horwich was found by pure luck when a gang of men warming themselves around a wood fire at the foot of the hill were distrubed by a noise. Thinking that there was danger at hand they threw earth and stone of a black nature onto the fire and then hid some distance away. The alert proved false and on returning to their fire they saw that the 'black stones' were glowing brightly. This incident gave the name Coal Fires Lane to a route leading to Mr Peak's Tile Works.

Fairclough's Smithy, Emmet Street, Horwich – 1908. The Smithy was situated where the British Legion Club now stands.

CHAPTER 19
Hospitals

Fall Birch Hospital

In an effort to prevent the spread of infectious diseases the Lancashire County Council, by Order dated 2nd November 1899, amalgamated Horwich, Blackrod and Westhoughton as a hospital district with fifteen members to be nominated by the respective Councils in the ratio of Horwich 7, Westhoughton 6 and Blackrod 2.

At the first meeting of the Hospital Committee held on the 7th May 1900 a decision was taken to purchase a site at

Fall Birch belonging to Mr J B Crompton on which a hospital was to be constructed. The foundation stone was laid almost three years later, on the 23 April 1903, by the Committee Chairman Mr J Unsworth.

Following completion and having been declared fit for the reception of patients, Fall Birch Hospital was formally opened on the 9th March 1905. Mr J Unsworth who had officiated at the foundation stone laying ceremony also presided at the opening.

Entrance, Fall Birch Hospital.

The Scarlet Ward, Fall Birch Hospital.

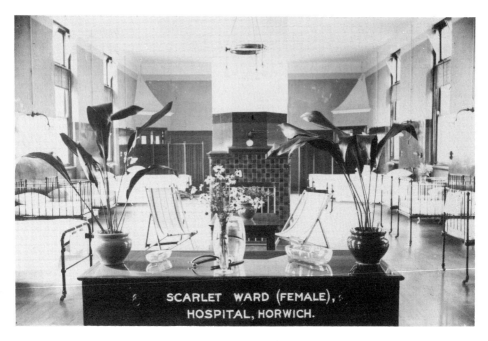

Interior Scarlet Ward (Female), Fall Birch Hospital.

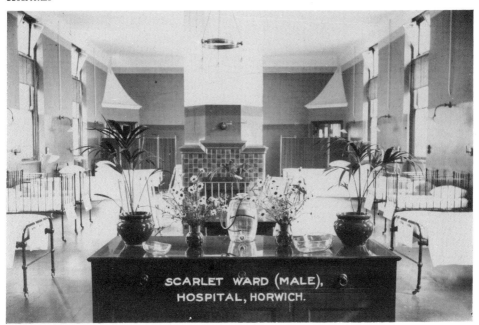

Interior Scarlet Ward (Male), Fall Birch Hospital.

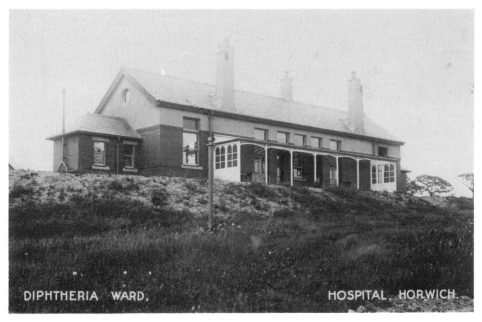

The Diphtheria Ward, Fall Birch Hospital.

The Typhoid Ward (Female), Fall Birch Hospital.

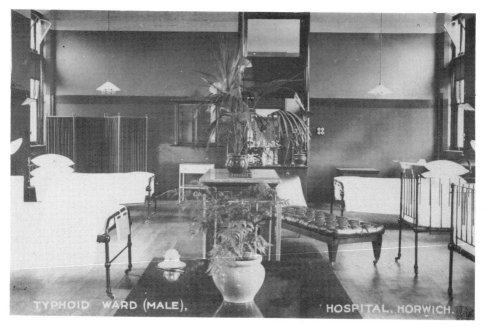

The Typhoid Ward (Male), Fall Birch Hospital.

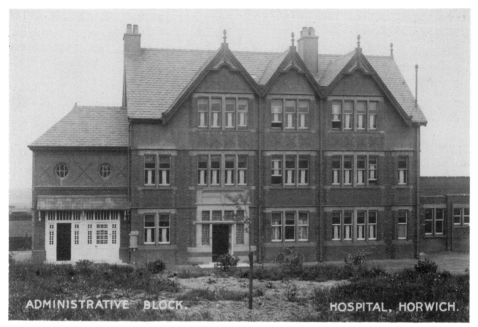

The Administrative Block, Fall Birch Hospital

L & Y Cottage Hospital, Brunel Street, Horwich.

The Lancashire and Yorkshire Cottage Hospital

Henry Yates Thompson, a Director of the Lancashire and Yorkshire Railway Company, provided a cottage hospital together with finance for its staffing as a gift to Horwich in memory of his father. During the First World War the hospital facilities were made available to wounded servicemen.

Inside L & Y Cottage Hospital.

CHAPTER 20
Sport and Leisure

At one time the majority of social activities were organised by the church but as Horwich became more and more industralised the various firms also began to provide sporting facilities and leisure pursuits for their workers.

People who work hard need an outlet to relieve the pressure and stress. Sport and leisure provide a 'safety valve' in this respect and can restore the mental and physical imbalance created by long hours of toil.

The sport and leisure activities enjoyed by Horwichers in those bygone days are at least as diverse as their modern counterparts, even taking account of television and electronic wizardry.

It is only possible to include a small selection of photographs and ephemera in the category of sport and leisure. Nevertheless it is considered that they represent a true reflection of Horwich at play in yesteryear.

Horwich Central Football Club – Circa 1910.

Lee Lane, Horwich – Circa 1897. It is not known what event is being celebrated although the bunting across the street, the fancy dress costume and Sunday best clothes suggest that it is a time for public festivity. The street trader also seems to be doing brisk business. A comparison between the Craven Heifer shown here and the present day building which once bore the same name confirms that this is an earlier pub. Other properties shown are, from left to right, the station master's house, Sharples Row and Holden's Row. Between the 'Perfection' advert and the Craven Heifer was the entrance to Horwich Railway Station.

HORWICH MUSICAL SOCIETY

PRESIDENT : JAMES SEDDON, ESQ.

The Messiah

(Handel)

WEDNESDAY, DECEMBER 15th, 1948

in the

VICTORIA   METHODIST   CHURCH

at 7-0 p.m.

Artistes :

MYRA   AINSWORTH............Soprano
LILIAN FARNELL...............Contralto
EDWARD   BEBBINGTON.........Tenor
ENOCH   STANYER.................Bass

: A U G M E N T E D   C H O R U S :

Conductor...............Harold Williams
At the Organ............Fred Partington

P R O G R A M M E   ::   ::   6d.

The Proceeds of this Concert are being
devoted to Local Charities.

St. John Ambulance Brigade,
HORWICH DIVISION

Twenty-Seventh Annual

DANCE

will be held in the

MECHANICS' INSTITUTE,

Horwich,

ON

NEW YEAR'S EVE 1930.

Music Supplied by

Reg Cameron's Rhythmn Boys.

—·▷+⁖∘⁖+◁·—

Efficient M·C s Will Be In Attendance.

Dancing from 8 p.m.until 2 a.m.

Spot Dances etc,

TICKETS 2/- Each.

Div.Supt.W FARNWORTH.

Sgt.J.TURTON.Hon Sec,

Horwich Prize Medal Morris Men – Harry Morris, Leader – Circa 1900.

Procession passing the Crown Hotel, Chorley New Road, Horwich – Circa 1908.

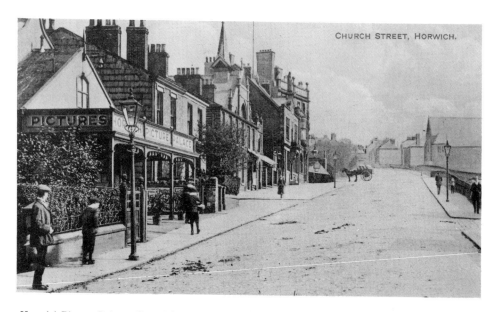

Horwich Picture Palace, Church Street, Horwich – Circa 1910. Horwich Picture Palace, seen on the left, had a corrugated iron roof which did nothing for the acoustics of the building during heavy rain or hail. Conversely, the strong sun made the inside uncomfortably hot and on these occasions the usherette sprayed a floral scented mist over the audience to cool and sweeten the atmosphere.

Chorley New Road Picture House – Circa 1920.

Horwich Mechanics Institute – Inside the gymnasium – Circa 1900. It seems as if the noble art of fencing was taught judging by the face guards and swords above the clock.

Horwich Cattle Fair.

The 39th

Annual Fair

FOR THE SALE OF

HORSES, CATTLE, SHEEP, &c.,

WILL BE HELD ON

Wednesday, Oct. 1st, 1913,

At the UPPER END of the Town.

LIST OF PRIZES.

	s.	d.
Best Dairy Cow—to Calve within two months of Fair (Open Class)	10	0
Second Best do. do. do.	5	0
Best Dairy Cow in milk (Open Class)	10	0
Second Best do. do.	5	0
Best Heifer in Calf or Milk—not to have more than four broad teeth up (Open)	10	0
Second Best do. do.	5	0
Best Fat Cow (Farmers only)	10	0
Second Best do.	5	0
Fat Bull or Bullock (Farmers only)	10	0
Pen of Sheep, not less than 8 (Farmers only)	10	0
Pen of Sheep, not less than 8 (Open Class 4 miles radius)	10	0
Best Mare or Gelding for Agricultural Purposes ...	10	0
Second Best do. do. do.	5	0
Best 2-year-old Gelding or Filly for Agricultural Purposes	10	0
Best 1-year-old do. do. do.	10	0
Best Weaning Colt or Filly for Agricultural Purposes...	10	0
Second Best do. do. do. ...	5	0
Best Roadster Mare or Gelding	10	0

Poster for Horwich Cattle Fair 1.10.1913.

Horwich Parish Church Football Team. The tall man extreme left is Walter Farnworth, Superintendent of St John Ambulance, Horwich.

The Pavilion, Recreation Ground, Horwich (Ramsbottom Road runs behind the Pavilion). The Lancashire and Yorkshire Railway Company opened a recreation ground, bounded on two sides by Chorley New Road and Ramsbottom Road, on the 23rd April, 1892. A cricket match was played to mark the opening. Other facilities provided at the recreation ground were two bowling greens, tennis courts and a children's playground.

Victoria Wesleyan Methodists Football Team – 1910.

Horwich Cricket Ground – 1906.

Recreation Ground, Horwich – 1912.

Grace Street, Horwich, decorated to celebrate the Silver Jubilee of King George V, 1935.

Ramsbottom Road, Horwich – 1930. Ramsbottom Road is named after John Ramsbottom a consultant engineer to the L & Y Railway who was largely responsible for initially setting up Horwich Locomotive Works.

Entrance to L & Y Recreation Ground, Ramsbottom Road, Horwich – Circa 1915. View across the cricket field with the tennis courts visible in the background.

The Saddle Inn bowling green, Silverwell Street, Horwich.

CHAPTER 21
Tunes of Glory

Public ceremonies, processions of witness, dances, gala days and sporting events are always complemented by the attendance of a Brass Band. There is something stirring and at the same time reassuring about the unique sound of brass instruments whether playing martial music or Christmas carols.

Over the years Horwich has boasted a number of fine bands which have included some notable musicians. Band practice was all important if there was to be any hope of success in the Brass Band Contests held in May, July and September at Belle Vue Gardens, Manchester.

Competition was extremely fierce and it was no mean achievement to carry off one of the coveted prizes, particularly against such contestants as the Black Dyke Mills Band, the Brighouse and Rastrick Band and the Wingates Temperance Band. Horwich Old Prize Band won the 1911 July competition with 'Il Matrimonio Segreto' (D Cimarso) and were second in July 1912 with 'Simon Boccanegra' (G Verdi).

The Lancashire and Yorkshire Railway had its own brass band which did not enjoy much success and so the company decided to invest in improving its per-

Horwich Old Prize Band 1916.

The L & Y Loco Prize Band – 1912.

formance by the introduction of new blood. The formation of the new band was proposed in 1912 by George Hughes who was then the Chief Mechanical Engineer for the L & Y Railway. Auditions were held and only one member of the existing L & Y Band was successful, the others being recruited from established bands. Thus the old L & Y Band became the Horwich Railway Mechanics' Institute Band. In 1915 the Horwich RMI Band came second to Foden's Motor Works Band in the September Championships. The test piece was 'Il Furioso' (Donizetti). Fate then took a hand when several members of Foden's Band were

sacked following a strike. These men joined the Horwich RMI Band who in September 1916 carried off the Championship Trophy beating Foden's Band into second place with their rendition of 'La Traviata' (Verdi). The band conductor on both these winning occasions was Mr J A Greenwood who later moved on to Creswell Colliery Band.

The crowning glory for the Horwich RMI Band came on the 23rd September 1922 when they won the prestigious Crystal Palace Trophy effectively making them champions of Great Britain and the Colonies.

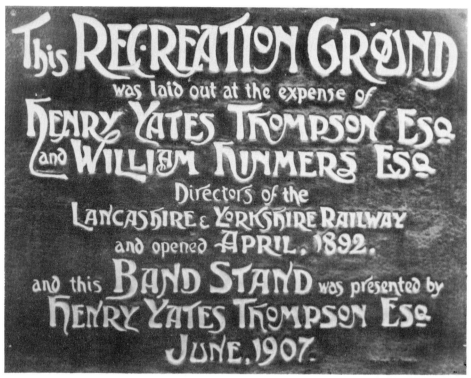

The Plaque from the Bandstand.

Horwich RMI Band with the Crystal Palace Grand Challenge Trophy which they won on the 23rd September 1922.

Close up of the Crystal Palace Grand Challenge Cup.

CHAPTER 22
The Prince's Arcade, Lee Lane, Horwich

Harrison Court once stood opposite the bottom of Brownlow Road and was demolished to be replaced by an arcade containing a theatre, a shopping centre and a billiard hall.

Prince's Theatre was opened on the 14th September 1895 when 1,400 people attended to see a performance of 'Babes in the Wood'. The manager at this time was a Mr J Greenhalgh of Bolton but the place is best remembered in connection with his successor, Johnny Holland, who ran it from just before the First World War until his death in the 1920's. Apart from his managerial responsibilities, Johnny Holland was a showman in his own right. To liven up performances he sometimes threw a live duck into the audience. He was always impeccably dressed having been known frequently to appear dressed in one smart suit in the morning, changing into another at lunchtime in the flat which he occupied above the Central Reform Club.

Prince's Arcade with Livesey's Wagonette standing outside – 1920.

152

Prince's Arcade showing Frank Hart's Cycle Shop – 1930.

Mr and Mrs Johnny Holland.

The couple in theatrical costume.

Two brothers, Jack and Sammy Marsden, successively held the job as projectionist at the Prince's Theatre, Sammy taking over from Jack in 1916. During the First World War photographs of local serving soldiers were flashed on the screen and any relative of the servicemen who was in the audience at the time was refunded the entrance fee and awarded a prize. In addition, a packet of cigarattes was dispatched to the soldier's Unit. Sammy Marsden worked at the Theatre until 1951 and saw the transition from 'silent films' to 'talkies' which took place about 1931. In the changeover period Sammy helped in the formation of a band entitled 'Abie Platt and his Syncopated Ten'.

Abie who was no mean pianist failed in an attempt to beat the world non-stop playing record which then stood at 44 hours. He collapsed after 34¼ hours continuous playing. Other performers at the Prince's included 'The Scholeys – Famous Ugly Sisters' a pair of female impersonators.

Prince's Theatre – Albie's Syncopating Ten on stage at the theatre. Standing to the left is Sammy Marsden.

The famous ugly sisters (George and Tom) photographed in October 1926.

Shop premises in the arcade changed hands fairly frequently and numbering among the tenants were Jackson's Fireplaces, Price's Cake Shop, Frank Hart's Cycle Shop and Mr Hignett's Antique Shop. The arcade was a meeting place for local youths, particularly during the inclement weather, and much time was 'mis-spent' in the Billiard Hall.

After Johnny Holland's death in the 1920's his wife continued to run the business. The theatre was gas lit until the late 1930's and the old gas engine interrupted many a performance while noisly discharging exhaust fumes via the pipe which poked through the roof. No doubt the installation of electricity provided a welcome relief.

Prince's Arcade – just prior to demolition.

Throughout the Second World War the Prince's Theatre, like the 'Folies Bergere', never closed. When the air raid siren sounded the audience was invited to shelter in the cellar of the premises, although many stayed in their seats and carried on watching the film heedless of any danger.

The Central Billiard Hall Company of

Burnley eventually purchased the theatre building and the whole complex was demolished in 1962.

Even though Johnny Holland's association with the Prince's Theatre ceased on his death he was affectionately remembered for many years thereafter and right up to the building complex being pulled down it was always known as "Johnny's".

The Billiard Hall after the last frame had been played.

Demolition of Prince's Theatre Complex – 1962.

CHAPTER 23
Highways and Byways

The Old Turnpike Road

As methods of road building improved the routes through Horwich were constructed at lower levels. The early roads such as the Old Hoghton Causey followed a high contour across the moor. With the establishment of the Bolton and Nightingale Turnpike Trust in 1763 a roadway linking Adlington and Bolton was improved for use and toll cottages were erected, one near the Crown Hotel at Horwich and one at Doffcocker in

Bolton. The old toll cottages had windows on all sides so that traffic could be seen from whichever direction it approached. This road was considerably straightened and widened in 1785 and eventually became Chorley Old Road. There were several coaching houses along the route of the old turnpike road including the Horwich Moorgate Inn (Blundell Arms) and the Black Bull Hotel. Chorley Old Road has been improved many times over the years and

Bob's Smithy, Chorley Old Road – Circa 1930. The old smithy can be seen at the corner of Old Kiln Lane. (recognisable by its tall chimney).

Scant Row – 1890. The largest of these cottages, standing to the right of the picture, was once occupied by a veterinary surgeon.

during road widening in the 1930's the old smithy opposite the Bob's Smithy pub was demolished.

A complicated network of subsidiary roads linked the old turnpike road with properties on the hillside.

Hart's Houses, Horwich – 1915. Hart's Houses is a row of seven cottages developed from a building lease granted in 1852. The cottages are on the site of Hodgkinson Wood. This early photograph shows the lane leading from Mill Lane with Rockhaven Castle on the skyline.

Edge Hill Road, Horwich – 1912

View from Horwich Parish Church – 1907. The houses at Edge Hill can be seen in the centre with Wilderswood Mill behind and Rockhaven Castle on the horizon.

Sparrow Park, Brownlow Road, Horwich – 1890. At the bottom of Brownlow Road, near to the junction with Lee Lane is a small area of trees and grassland known locally as Sparrow Park. A row of cottages previously occupied the site and this view shows the demolition of those cottages. After the First World War a captured field gun was placed in the park as a memorial but this was taken to be melted down for armaments during the 1939-45 World War.

Brownlow Road, Horwich – 1919.

Lee Lane, Horwich – Circa 1935.

Lee Lane, Horwich – 1929

Crown Hotel, Horwich – Circa 1900.

The earlier Crown Hotel, Horwich – Circa 1880.

Scholes Bank, Horwich – Circa 1895.

Pike Road, Horwich (now Lever Park Avenue) – Circa 1905.

Chorley New Road

Chorley New Road was constructed in 1829 and followed a more direct route between Horwich and Bolton. The road was originally intended to facilitate the carriage of unfinished textiles into Horwich for bleaching, etc., and their return for sale in the Manchester Markets.

Chorley New Road, Horwich – Circa 1910.

View of Chorley New Road from the Black Dog Hotel – 1910.

Winter Hey Lane and Black Dog Hotel – 1930. Winter Hey Lane was once known as Dog Lane and the Black Dog Hotel was known as 'The Greyhound'.

Winter Hey Lane, showing the old Post Office – 1912.

Chorley New Road from the railway bridge, photograph taken during the 1940 snow storm.

The Roundabout, Scholes Bank, Horwich – Circa 1950.

Tram at the Crown Terminus, Horwich – Circa 1940.

Victoria Crescent, Horwich – 1926.

Chorley New Road, Horwich – 1914. The 'Tram Shed' can be seen on the left with a group of people outside.

1940 snow storm, looking towards Rockhaven Castle.

Chorley New Road, Horwich – Circa 1920.

The latest road to be constructed through Horwich and the nearest to sea-level was the M61 Manchester to Preston Motorway, built in the late 1960's.

CHAPTER 24
Horwich Locomotive Works

The calm before the storm

In 1881 the population of Horwich was 3,761 and this number had varied little over the preceding fifty years. The highway rate was fourpence in the £ (2p) and these dues were collected by a local farmer whose approach was always known well in advance by the sound of his clogs on the cobblestones. There were 900 houses in the village at the time, rents were relatively cheap and there was no reason to suspect that the future held any surprises in store.

No one in Horwich could have been expected even to guess that within the next decade an industrial explosion would occur with the arrival of Horwich Locomotive Works. This event was destined not only to upgrade the place to town status by increasing the population to 12,850 but to touch most Horwichers' lives for nearly a century thereafter.

Choosing a site

It was on the 19th March 1884 that John Ramsbottom, a consultant engineer to the Lancashire and Yorkshire Railway Company, informed the board of directors that their locomotive works at Miles Platting was too small to provide proper repair facilities for the company's rolling stock. Extra premises were urgently needed if the business was to remain competitive. He recommended that a site for new workshops be obtained. The overriding considerations in its selection should be a central situation, good supplies of water and cheap coal and a readily available workforce.

Several possible sites were examined and none proved entirely suitable until the board were informed of the proposed sale of a 350 acre site in Horwich. Elias Dorning, surveyor for the L & YR, examined the site along with Ramsbottom and William Barton Wright, the chief locomotive superintendent. They were suitably impressed and on reporting back to the directors Dorning was authorised to bid up to £65,000 for the property when it came up for auction at the Mitre Hotel, Manchester, on 27th May 1884. In the event the company managed to secure the land for a bargain £36,000!

Development of the site

There were several preliminary matters to be attended to before the site could be properly developed. A temporary rail connection was needed to link the site with the main railway routes, a large hill on the site at 'Old Hart's farm' was to be levelled, several footpaths needed to be diverted and the Manchester Corporation agreed to alter the course of the Thirlmere pipeline at L & YR expense.

It was intended to start building the office and workshop accommodation in the Spring of 1885 and preparation of the plans and specifications began in earnest. William Barton Wright played an important part in the design of the works, submitting various plans including one for an office building with a clock tower. Incidently, the clock tower was never

View across Horwich from Chorley New Road – Circa 1880.

constructed. In addition to laying plans for the works, Wright was concerned about providing accommodation for the workforce. He estimated that upwards of 1,400 people would be employed at the works when they were completed.

Accommodation for the workforce

Some 200 acres of the site were sold off on chief rents for building purposes and a network of streets was planned in close proximity to the works. The streets were planned to have a width of twelve to sixteen yards and included Victoria Road, named after Queen Victoria and several others named after famous inventors or railway personages such as Arkwright, Brunel, Fox, Hawkshaw, Nasmyth and Stephenson. This transaction recouped not only the £36,000 cost of the site but a large part of the expenditure on the workshops as well.

Hawkshaw Street, Horwich – 1902. Hawkshaw Street is named after John Hawkshaw (born 1811) one of the most important L & YR Engineers.

Victoria Road, Horwich – 1906

Fox Street, Horwich – 1900. Fox Street is named after Charles Douglas Fox (born 1840) who was jointly responsible with James Brunlees for the Mersey Railway Tunnel and many other projects.

Labour disputes

Things did not always run smoothly during the course of erection of the works. Bad weather and labour disputes caused frequent interruptions to the building programme. There was terrible ill feeling between the English and Irish labourers on the site because the latter were paid one halfpenny per hour less. The situation became so serious that extra police were drafted into the town in an attempt to keep order between the rival factions.

One evening a group of Irishmen beat up a one armed Englishman at the Craven Heifer pub. This incident was the spark for a series of running battles along Lee Lane and Winter Hey Lane. About 10.30 pm the forces re-grouped. The Irishmen were assembled in Summer Street when the two sides clashed again. A fierce fight ensued involving bricks, pokers and bottles. One Irishman is reported to have been seen galloping round with a scythe until a well aimed brick put him out of action. Police reinforcements which had been held in reserve at the Public Hall eventually managed to restore peace. A number of those involved were subsequently gaoled without the option of a fine for their part in the affray.

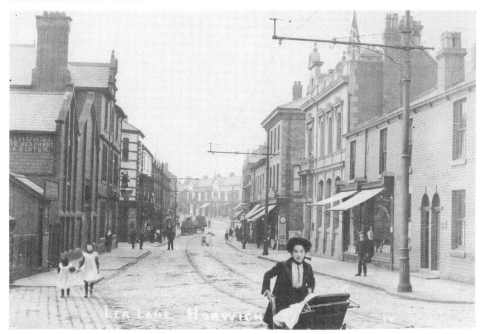

The Craven Heifer can be seen on the left with a large ornate lamp outside.

Winter Hey Lane, Horwich – 1910.

William Paterson whose father was licensee of The Crown Hotel at the turn of the century, recollected a strike at the locomotive works in 1906 which lasted for twelve weeks. During this time free meat was provided by Anyon Kay a local butcher and vegetables were donated by several greengrocers, these were used to make soup for the children of the striking workers.

In those days William, then 10 years old, used to get up at 4.30 a.m. each morning so that when the pub opened at 5.45 a.m., he could supply workers with rum and coffee before they caught the tram.

Labour Demonstration, Horwich – June 1906.

Completion of the Works

Horwich Locomotive Works was in full operation by 1892 having been under development since the Spring of 1885. One of the first buildings constructed was the 'erecting shop' a cathedral like edifice measuring some 1,520 feet long and 118 feet wide. There were three bays to the shop with space sufficient to accommodate up to 90 engines and 30 tenders. The enormity of this building is illustrated by the fact that twenty 30-ton overhead cranes from Hetherington and Company of Manchester were installed, four in each of the five sections of the shop.

Miniature railway

Eight miniature railway engines, named respectively Robin, Wren, Dot, Fly, Wasp, Midget, Mouse and Bee, were either purchased or constructed to convey materials around the site on seven and a half miles of 18 inch gauge railway track.

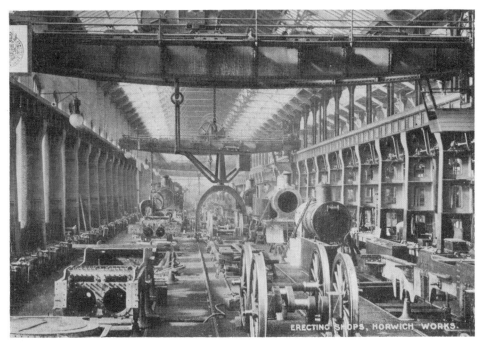

Erecting Shop at Horwich Locomotive Works – 1906.

18in gauge engine hauling locomotive boiler – Dot – at Horwich Locomotive Works.

Sir John Frederick Audley Aspinall

William Barton Wright who had worked so hard to achieve the establishment of Horwich Locomotive Works resigned from the L & YR on the 23rd June 1886. In addition to the completion of the erecting shop – construction of the office block, boiler shop, smithy, forge and foundry, stores building, etc, also was well under way. Wright was succeeded by John Audley Frederick Aspinall who was then 35 years of age, a brilliant engineer and a former pupil of John Ramsbottom.

Horwich Locomotive Works – 1905

Horwich Mechanics Institute

Aspinall quickly appraised himself of the situation with Horwich Locomotive Works and soon began to make his presence felt. He wrote to the L & YR Board on the 22nd November 1886 recommending the urgent introduction of a premium apprentice scheme the monies from which would fund the cost of providing a mechanics' institute. This suggestion obviously carried weight with the company in that both plans were approved. Horwich Mechanics' Institute was designed by Henry Shelmadine & Co. in 1887. It cost £3,140 to build and was officially opened on the 15th December 1888. The institute provided places for up to ninety students a week who were charged nominal fees provided that they attended at least twenty-one classes in each subject, otherwise the fees were doubled.

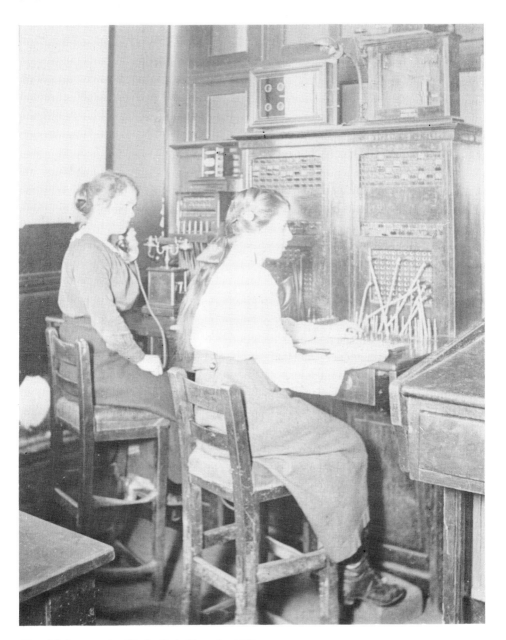

Horwich Locomotive Works Switchboard – 1902.

Horwich Locomotive Works Drawing Office – 1902.

Horwich Mechanics' Institute – Circa 1890.

LANCASHIRE AND YORKSHIRE RAILWAY.

Mechanics' Institute, Horwich.

STUDENTS' FOURTH ANNUAL

SUMMER ✣ EXCURSION

On Friday, July 3rd, 1891,

TO

LONDON.

JAMES T. TATLOW, Hon. Sec.

Lancashire and Yorkshire Railway.

MECHANICS' INSTITUTE, HORWICH.

STUDENTS' FIFTH ANNUAL

Summer ✿ Excursion

ON FRIDAY, JULY 1st, 1892,

TO

LONDON AND CHATHAM DOCKYARD.

JAMES T. TATLOW, HON. SEC.

MECHANICS' INSTITUTE AND TECHNICAL SCHOOL,
HORWICH.

LECTURE BY

Dr. W. T. GRENFELL, C.M.G.,

ON

" Midst Ice and Snow in Labrador."

Friday, October 10th, 1924, at 7=30 p.m.

RESERVED SEAT No.

FLETCHER, TYPS.

The 'Samuel Fielden Wing'

Not content with the facilities afforded at the Mechanics Institute, Aspinall continued to press for their extension which was eventually made possible by a gift from the widow of a former director of the L & YR, Samuel Fielden. A large hall was added with seating for 900 persons, a library, reading rooms and class rooms. Part of the extension was named the 'Samuel Fielden Wing' and the additional building was opened in October 1895.

Horwich Mechanics' Institute – Circa 1902. This view shows the extension and the Samuel Fielden Wing added in 1895 can be seen in the foreground.

The L & Y Arms

Shelmadine & Co. were also responsible for the design of the L & Y Arms, a dining hall which was built at a cost of £1,627 on the corner of Gooch Street and Chorley New Road. Apparently there was a possibility that the premises would be used as a pub but this never materialised.

Chorley New Road, Horwich – 1910. The Mechanics' Institute can be seen on the right.

L & Y Cafe – Circa 1902.

Chorley New Road, Horwich – Circa 1907. The distinctive L & Y Cafe can be seen back right of photo.

Horwich Locomotive Works Canteen (interior view) – Circa 1902.

Chief Mechanical Engineers (CME's)

John A F Aspinall remained as chief mechanical engineer at Horwich for ten years and left to take up appointment as general manager of the L & YR on the 31st May 1899. During his stay at Horwich the Locomotive Works had been completed and 677 engines had come off the production line including a number built to Aspinall's own design.

In 1917 Aspinall received a knighthood for his services to the railway industry. He died aged 85 years at his London home on the 19th January 1937. Just three days later, on the 22nd January, he

Engine No 1394. A 4-4-2 Express Engine built at Horwich Locomotive Works on the 13th April 1899. The engine was in service until April 1927 under the L M S number 10303.

was to have been presented with the "James Watt Gold Medal" – the highest award in engineering.

Aspinall's departure from Horwich resulted in several internal promotions and the works manager, Henry Albert Hoy, replaced him as CME. When Hoy resigned in 1904 he was likewise succeeded by the works manager George Hughes.

Amalgamations

The L & YR and the London and North Western Railway (LNWR) had been tentatively discussing a merger since 1872 and by a series of agreements worked their separate operations fairly closely. Following the first world war amalgamation became the only means of ensuring the survival of the companies and they joined forces on the 1st January 1922, trading as LNWR.

On the 1st January, 1923, the LNWR was itself absorbed into a grouping of railway companies and became part of the London Midland and Scottish Railway Company (LMS).

Aerial view of Horwich Locomotive Works – Circa 1930.

Throughout this period George Hughes remained as CME at Horwich Locomotive Works but he took early retirement in 1925, at the age of sixty.

One development which contributed to this decision was that the power base within the company had been transferred from Horwich to Derby.

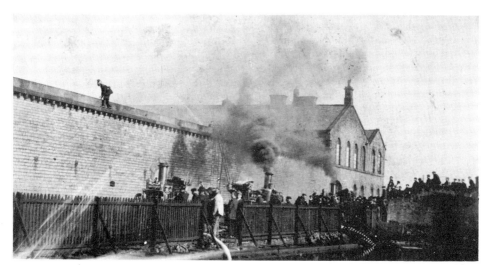

L & YR Fire fighting practice at Horwich – Circa 1909.

L & YR 'Merryweather' horse drawn fire appliance – Circa 1897.

The L & YR Fire Brigade

The L & YR maintained its own Fire Brigade at Horwich Locomotive Works which was equipped with a number of horse-drawn 'Merryweather' fire appliances. Fire fighting practice was held regularly and the equipment was main-tained in superb condition. As well as dealing with fires on railway property the Brigade assisted in tackling local out-breaks within reasonable travelling distance, although when 'The Bungalow' at Rivington was set alight on the 7th July 1913, the L & YR Brigade refused to attend because Rivington lay outside its area of operation.

Lancashire Constabulary – Horwich Section – 1916. This photograph was taken in the yard behind the police station. The officer in charge is believed to be Inspector Linaker.

Lancashire Constabularly – Horwich Section – Circa 1920. Inspector Ryder and his men pictured in the Mechanics' Institute with John McLean the Librarian.

Horwich Police

The first police force was introduced into Horwich during 1840 when three Lancashire County Constabulary officers, Sergeant Charles Wilson and Constables Dawson and Craig, were posted to take up duties in what was then Horwich village. Initially the policemen met a hostile reception from the local residents because they were seen as invaders of liberty but gradually their presence was accepted. In those early days there was no police station and the three officers were obliged to use their own homes for keeping prisoners. A 'lock-up' was eventually provided at Blackrod.

With the arrival of the Locomotive Works and the attendant steep rise in population the police establishment was also increased. A custom built police station was provided in Church Street during 1887.

Wartime

During both the first and second world wars Horwich Locomotive Works played an important part in the manufacture of tanks, munitions, etc., for the armed forces, and with so much of the male population away fighting at the front, a great deal of the war work was actually carried out by the women.

To honour those employees who gave their lives in the Great War, the L & YR erected a war memorial in front of the works. George Hughes (CME) unveiled the memorial on the 27th August 1921.

In recognition of Horwich's contribution to war effort in the 39/45 War the King and Queen visited the town on the 2nd May, 1940.

Horwich Victory Ball Celebration.

1914-1919.

‹•●•›

◄ SOUVENIR. ►

Mechanics' Institute, Horwich.   Wednesday, February 12th, 1919.

A PROUD RECORD.

THIS small town sent 1230 lads to " do their bit."   70 have made the supreme sacrifice.   44 suffered as Prisoners of War.
260 have been wounded—varying from one to four times.
50 have won Decorations—including D.S.O., Military Cross, Military Medal, D.C.M., and Belgian, French, Italian, and Serbian Decorations.
Three Nurses have secured the coveted Royal Red Cross.

All these, with those supplying Munitions, have helped to bring us Victory, and it is right and proper we should celebrate in a joyous manner.

JOE FLETCHER, Chairman.
FRANK BRINDLE, Secretary.
J. B. WRIGHT, Treasurer.

War Memorial

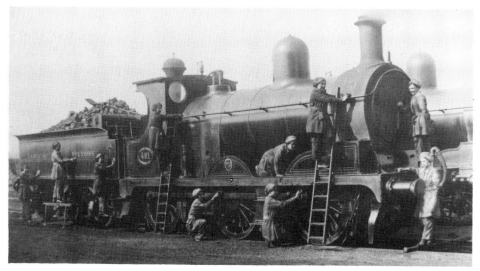

Engine cleaning Horwich Locomotive Works – 1915.

King George VI and Queen Elizabeth at Horwich Railway Station on their visit to the town – 2nd May 1940.

Post War Decline

After the second world war a whole series of events combined to diminish the importance of Horwich locomotive Works. Diesel powered trains and electrification schemes began to replace the steam locomotive, 'nationalisation' was introduced on the 1st January 1948 and the Beeching Report (1963) resulted in wholesale axeing of train services.

The last steam locomotive constructed at Horwich left the works on the 27th November 1957. A programme was then introduced for the manufacture of shunting diesels which lasted until the end of 1962. Responsibility was then further reduced to repairing engines and finally maintaining railway wagons.

The last train from Horwich Railway Station

The railway service to Horwich Station was a casualty of the 'Beeching axe' and the passenger train service was withdrawn on the 27th September 1965. Goods traffic continued to use the line until the 25th April 1966 and it was finally closed on the 30th January 1967.

The Closure of Horwich Locomotive Works

British Railways was fundamentally re-organised in the wake of the Beeching

The last train to leave Horwich Railway Station.

The Derelict Railway Station – 1969

cuts and although Horwich works escaped closure on this occasion, which was the fate of a number of other workshops, there was tremendous uncertainty about the future. Despite assurances from management and injections of cash to upgrade the facilities at the works there was a feeling of impending doom.

On the 18th February 1983, British Rail Engineering Limited (formed on the 1st January 1970) announced that Horwich Locomotive Works was to close at the end of the year. Protest marches and spirited trade union resistance failed to alter the decision and so at 1 pm on Friday, 23rd December, 1983 the last shift left the works and the gates were closed behind them.

Conclusion

Horwich Locomotive Works operated from November 1886 when the first six locomotives were taken in for repair until its closure at the end of 1983, a total of 97 years. Altogether, 1,830 steam locomotives, 169 diesel locomotives and five 18 inch gauge locomotives were built. In addition, some 50,000 locomotives were repaired over the first 76 year period.

The most significant benefits of the works are that for nearly a century it was the main source of employment for the people of Horwich and district. It gave them self respect as wage earners and helped to hold together the fabric of society through some very difficult times.

Horwich Locomotive Works – Circa 1960. The first locomotive a 2-4-2T No 1008 which left the works on the 20th February 1889 can be seen front right.

Workers leaving Horwich Locomotive Works – 1911.

Logo of Lancashire and Yorkshire Railway.

Bibliography

The following are the major works to which I have referred:–

The Lancashire & Yorkshire Railway (3 volumes)	–John Marshall
History of England	–G M Trevelyan
Baines History of Lancashire (Salford Hundred)	
History of Bolton	–P A Whittle
A Short History of Manchester and Salford	–F A Bruton
The Great Human Exploit	–Edited by J H Smith
History of Co-operation in Horwich (1862–1912)	–J Colbridge J Parr and W J Dale
From Affetside to Yarrow	–W D Billington
History of Horwich	–Thomas Hampson
History of Rivington	–Thomas Hampson
History of New Chapel, Horwich	–Francis George Collier
Horwich: The Historical Geography of a Lancashire Town	–B J Turton
Victoria Methodist Church, Horwich (1810–1960]	–John H Davis
St Mary's RC Church Horwich (1886-1986)	–G E Hester